FOOD FOR CANNIBALS

The motto of Vanuatu is 'In God we stand'.

Espiritu Santo

Aobe

Maéwo

Pentecost

Malakula

Efaté

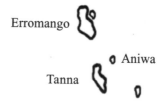

Erromango

Aniwa

Tanna

Anatomi

FOOD FOR CANNIBALS

The story of John Paton

Jim Cromarty

 EVANGELICAL PRESS

EVANGELICAL PRESS
Faverdale North Industrial Estate, Darlington, DL3 0PH,
England

Evangelical Press USA
P. O. Box 825, Webster, New York 14580, USA

e-mail: sales@evangelicalpress.org
web: http://www.evangelicalpress.org

First published 2004

British Library Cataloguing in Publication Data available

ISBN 0 85234 548 8

Printed and bound in Great Britain by Creative Print and Design
Wales, Ebbw Vale, South Wales.

Contents

Preface

Have you ever thought of becoming a missionary in some far away country? This book tells you the story of a great missionary – John Paton who took the good news concerning the Lord Jesus Christ to people who had no interest in the Saviour. John Paton faced vicious cannibals who killed and ate people without a care in the world. He trusted in God to protect him and died in Australia when very old.

There are people in the world today who have never heard of the Christ. We live amongst many people who only know the name of Jesus Christ as an oath when they swear.

Young people, there is a God who loves sinners; there is a God who sent his Son into this world to save sinners and he calls you to go to him and believe with all your heart and mind that not only *can* he save you from hell, but *will* save you if only you trust your future to him. We can't earn our salvation. Christ was punished in the place of his people when he hung upon that terrible Roman cross. He also lived a life of perfect obedience to God, his Father, something that we should have done, but can never do. When the Lord Jesus Christ went to the cross a great transaction took place – he took our sins upon himself so he could be punished by God in the place of his people, and he in turn gave us his righteousness.

I know one man who read a book about John Paton, possibly sixty-five or seventy years ago. He gave up his work on the farm and studied very hard to pass his exams. Then he moved to

Edinburgh where at the same time he studied theology, medicine and a third degree to gain the qualification to be a chemist. He then moved to South Africa where he preached Christ, assisted the sick and dispensed medicines. What a man! Yet he gave all the glory to God for giving him such mental ability. However, remember it all started by reading the story of John Paton.

Read this story and then ask yourself the question: 'Could I become a missionary like John Paton – willing to risk everything, even life itself for the Lord I love? May God bless each and every one who reads this book.

A 'thank you' to Joshua and Dion for their photos on each of the 'something to think about' pages.

Jim Cromarty

Dedication

To Dr Helen Ramsey
who spent a lifetime serving the Lord in India

The **New Hebrides** is now called **Vanuatu**. It is made up of 12 larger and 70 smaller islands and is situated S/E of the Solomon Islands in the SW Pacific.
Population in 2,000 = 190,417. **Capital** – Vila on the island of Efaté.
Official languages – Bislama (Pidgin English), English and French.

The largest Christian denomination is Protestant and within this Presbyterians have the most churches (around 400). These are mainly in the south islands where John Paton first evangelized.
31.7% of the population is said to be Evangelical. Most missionaries are from USA and Australia.

Operation World tells us that Christians played a major role in the gaining of independence and in subsequent governments. It also tells us that pioneer missionaries are still needed.

1
A pirate in the family

Young John Paton knew that very few people had an ancestor who had been a pirate. However he'd often heard his father tell the story of John's grandfather, who for a time had sailed with the cold-blooded Captain Paul Jones, as a member of his pirate crew. John knew the story by heart as he'd heard it so many times, but it was always exciting. The family would sit about the warm log and peat fire in the dining room and listen to the tales of long ago.

His grandfather had been forced to serve as a sailor on a British man-of-war. He had been captured by the French during one battle, and from there the fierce pirate, Captain Paul Jones, had forced him to become one of his crew.

Grandfather had a long, wide, white scar on his shoulder, where Captain Jones, in a fit of temper, had slashed him with a sword. The wound was deep and he had lost a lot of blood. Later he'd been able to escape from the pirate ship and make his way home to Scotland.

After his father had told the family the story, John's mother enjoyed telling them of her parents. Her father, William Rogerson, was a poor blacksmith, who had fallen in love with Janet Jardine. She had wealthy parents but they had died and her uncles were responsible for the care of her money. When William asked the uncles for Janet's hand in marriage, they refused as they didn't want their niece marrying a blacksmith. However, Janet wanted to marry William and plans were made for the wedding to take place.

One day, William and his friends mounted on their very swift horses, rode up to the home, where Janet jumped up behind William on his horse and away they went. Janet then married the blacksmith she loved and their life together was very happy.

When Janet asked for her parent's fortune her uncles quickly made plans for everything to be sold. They had decided to steal her money and move to America, where they would not be known.

When William heard about the auction, he once again mounted his fast horse, and set off for the sale. However, when he arrived, only the family Bible was left. Swiftly snatching the Bible and holding it under his arm, he returned to Janet.

John and his six sisters and four brothers really enjoyed hearing those stories, but it also thrilled their hearts when James, their dad, told them the story of the way he had met his wife, Janet. Dad had become a Christian when he was young, and in order to have a quiet time of prayer with God he found a place in a local wood.

Carrying his Bible and frequently a book of gospel poems by Ralph Erskine, called 'Gospel Sonnets', which he enjoyed reading aloud, he would go to the same quiet place. Carefully placing his hat on the bough of a nearby tree, James would kneel down and with eyes closed pray to God. He praised God for his goodness to him, confessed his love of God and after confessing his sins, thanked the Lord Jesus for dying on the cross for him. He prayed that the Holy Spirit would help him live a godly life.

Then he would open his Bible and read God's word. He loved his Bible, but more than anything else he loved the God who was revealed in the Scriptures. He spent time reading from a godly book, but often it was the poems of Erskine that he read aloud. By doing this he found himself learning by heart the words of Scripture and the writings of godly men and women.

In the woods James thought he was just alone with God. He had no idea that he was being watched by a lovely young lady. Janet was living with her great aunt and uncle, who had been nicknamed 'Old Adam and Eve' by all their friends. Janet had often watched the good-looking young stocking maker when he went into the woods for a quiet time with God.

One day she decided to follow him and when he knelt down to pray she quietly sneaked up to the place where he had hung his hat and moved it to another tree. When James had finished his time of worship and was ready to return to work he had to look for his hat. At first he thought he was absent minded and didn't remember where he had hung it.

The next time Janet moved his hat, he wasted quite a long time looking before he found it. She felt guilty for what she had done, so the next day pinned a note to his hat: 'She who stole your bonnet [hat] is ashamed of what she did; she has great respect for you, and asks that you pray for her, that she may become as good a Christian as you.'

Their father told his family that he thought an angel must have moved his hat. When he looked about, with the note in his hand and wondering who had been responsible, he saw 'an angel' in front of the cottage owned by 'Old Adam and Eve'. He said that she was walking along, swinging a pail of milk by her side.

It wasn't long before he made himself known to Janet. Their mum usually blushed and laughingly told her husband to be quiet. Often she teased her husband by asking why he went to that particular spot to be alone when he must have known that someone was moving his hat. John's mum and dad really loved each other.

Enjoyable as these stories were, it was the story of the Lord Jesus Christ that they loved above everything else. Young John had been born into a Christian family where Christ was the head of the house.

something to think about

1. John's father told John about the importance of prayer.
   There are five main points to his prayer time. The first one
   is 'he praised God for his goodness to him.' Can you find the
   other four points?

2. John's father loved to read the Bible more than any other
   book. Why is the Bible the best and most important book to
   read? The answer is in **2 Timothy 3:16.**

3. By reading the Bible and good Christian books, John's
   father found himself learning by heart the words of Scripture and the writings of godly men.
   Why do you think it is so important to do this when you are
   young?

2
Growing up

John was born on 24 May 1824 in a farmhouse at Braehead, near Dumfries in Scotland. In those days almost all babies were born at home. John's father, James, had a small workshop at one end of his house where warm, woollen stockings were manufactured. In the cold weather, woollen stockings helped the ladies keep warm. These were usually sold in Hawick and Dumfries.

John was given the middle name of 'Gibson' after a local, wealthy farmer who was a friend of the family. When John was able to walk, he often made his way to the Gibson's mansion where the farmer's wife would play with him.

When he turned five the family moved to Torthorwald which was a busy village. Many local people worked on the farms, while others made leather shoes for wealthy people or wooden clogs for labourers to wear. Cloth making was an important local industry and many people were involved in weaving cloth for clothing or, like John's father, warm, woollen stockings.

The village also had a mill where the local farmers had their corn ground for flour. There were also coopers who made barrels which were used to store sugar, flour, potatoes and other produce. They were also used to store alcohol. The blacksmith helped make these barrels, by shaping metal bands to hold the timber together.

Their three-roomed house had a thatched roof which was replaced each year. The building had stone walls between the solid oak beams which were fixed into the ground. The stones were cemented together using sand, clay and lime.

At one end was their father's workshop, where five or six men worked hard, weaving the stockings. The middle room was Mum and Dad's bedroom. In this room there was a bed, a small table and a chair. This was the room where their father would go for a quiet time of prayer and reading the Scriptures. Everyone knew that when Dad had 'shut the door', they were to be quiet.

The third room was Mum's room. It was the dining room, kitchen, living room and bedroom for the children – all in one room! Around the large wooden beds Mum had hung curtains to give privacy. On the beds were bright covers made by their mother.

The room had an open log and peat fire where the family gathered at night for many happy hours.

The children's mother had a garden both in their house block and across the road. There she grew fresh vegetables for the family and flowers which she used to brighten the home.

Each day, in the morning and evening, John's father would take down the large family Bible and call the family together for a time of worship. This was a time when the Scriptures were read and explained, psalms were sung, and prayer offered to God. No matter what was happening, everyone was expected to meet with the family for this time of worship. It was in the home that John, realising that he was a sinner, came to trust in the Lord Jesus Christ for the forgiveness of his sins and salvation.

John's mother and father longed to see their children serving God, especially as their father was not able to become a minister of the gospel. On the day John was born, both his mother and father spent time in prayer, thanking God for their son and solemnly giving him back to God. They prayed that the day would come when John would serve the Lord on the mission field. Their prayers were answered in a wonderful way.

Even as a young boy John felt that Jesus was calling him to missionary work. When they were older not only did John serve the Lord Jesus in the New Hebrides but two of his brothers served Jesus Christ as ministers in the Church.

Often the children heard their parents praying aloud in their own bedroom, that each of the children might become godly people, faithfully serving God.

When one of the children had to be punished, it was carried out with care. Their father would explain why they were to be punished, and after prayer for wisdom in the punishment to administer, did what he believed to be correct.

Standing on a hill nearby John could see church spires, and the roofs of houses in Dumfries about four miles away. Also in view was the shining white sand of Solway.

Turning around he could see a river wending its way through the many farms and villages in the district. In the distance were castle ruins, including Lochmaben castle which was once the home of the Scottish hero, Robert the Bruce. Another well known ruin he could see was Caerlaverock Castle. At night after their meal and family worship, the family would sit about the open fire and listen to John's father telling many exciting stories about the battles that were fought in the area.

Looking back over Torthorwald, John could see the many homes, the Parish Church, manse, school and a graveyard which dated back 500 years.

The Paton family didn't attend the local Presbyterian Church, but each Sunday walked the four miles to Dumfries, where they attended the Reformed Presbyterian Church.

Growing up in Torthorwald was exciting for the Paton children.

something to think about

1. On the day John was born his parents 'gave him back to God'. This means that they asked God to use John in any way he thought best. **Read 1 Samuel 1:20-24.** Here Hannah gives her son back to the Lord. What was his name?

2. John and his family had daily family worship which included prayer. In **Matthew 6:9-13** Jesus gives us a clear pattern concerning what we should pray for. Try to learn this prayer – called 'The Lord's Prayer' – it is a good pattern to follow.

3. Daily Dad would 'shut the door.' Think about what that means?
   In **Matthew 6:5-8 we are told that when we pray we are to 'close the door'.**
   How else can we 'close or shut the door'? It is difficult to talk to God when there is a lot of noise going on around us. How can we keep out thoughts that may distract us when we read and pray?

3
Christian living

Family life centred about the Lord Jesus, who was Lord of the Paton home. Each Sunday John's father, accompanied by those of his family who were able, walked to their Church where they praised and gave thanks to God for their salvation. Sunday was a special day for the family, and was known as 'The Sabbath' or 'The Lord's Day'. In forty years John's father only missed three worship services.

On one occasion, the snow was so deep he couldn't make his way along the pathway and was forced to return home.

The second time was also in winter when the pathway was covered with ice and was so slippery, that after several falls he returned home fearing that he might injure himself if he went any further. The pathway rising from a creek was so slippery that he was forced to slowly crawl along on his hands and knees.

The third occasion was when there was an outbreak of cholera in Dumfries. John's father didn't fear the disease and intended making his way to Dumfries for worship. However, some of the citizens of Torthorwald approached John's mother, asking her to persuade her husband to stay home for a week as they didn't want cholera breaking out in their village. This was not necessary though as before he heard their request, he had decided to remain at home and so help prevent the spread of the disease.

Many families in Scotland made Sunday a rather dull day, even making their homes dark by pulling down the blinds. For the Patons the Lord's Day was a joyful day as it reminded them of the resurrection of their Saviour, the Lord Jesus Christ.

Each Sunday John's father would set off for the four mile walk to Dumfries where they attended worship. Usually the Paton family met other families making their way to Dumfries for worship and as they walked along the discussion was mostly about God's wonderful salvation in Jesus Christ.

One subject that thrilled John's heart was the discussions he heard about the return of the Lord Jesus. He also showed a lot of interest in reports about mission work throughout the world, and early in his life he began to think that this was how he would serve God – as a missionary to the heathen people in the recently discovered parts of the world.

During the service, John and his brothers and sisters would take notes of the sermon. His mother found it difficult to get to worship each Lord's Day as she had small children. Sometimes she was offered a ride in a horse drawn sulky, but usually she waited at home until the family returned. After their meal she would be told of the service and all that the minister had preached. John and his brothers and sisters were able to take out their notes and from them make sure Mum heard all that happened. Frequently John's father would ask questions to make sure the children understood what they had heard.

After their evening meal, father would take the Bible for Family Worship. This would be followed by a discussion on a catechism question and answer. They used 'The Shorter Catechism.' Following this a Christian book was opened and everyone took turns in reading aloud the next section. Every-one enjoyed hearing the reading of John Bunyan's 'Pilgrim's Progress'. Often they listened to reports of the exciting mission work being carried out overseas.

Not only did John hear the truth of God's word from his parents, he also saw them living the Christian life. He was also to learn that the God his parents loved and served was the God of the 'impossible'.

John attended the Torthorwald village school. The teacher was Mr Smith who had a good reputation as a Christian and a teacher, although sometimes he was cruel to his students. The school was for both the rich and poor, as parents valued education and realized that school attendance encouraged character building. Mr Smith had constructed an extra room at the school where boarders could live during the week.

Mr Smith knew that John's parents were not wealthy, and when he saw that John was in need of some new clothing he bought some for him.

One night when his father was 'taking the books' – conducting family worship – something happened that John would remember for the rest of his life.

As the family was kneeling in prayer, Mr Smith quietly lifted the door latch and placed the bundle of clothes inside the door. When worship was concluded the family was surprised at what they found. John saw this as God providing what he needed! The family knew that their God was the God and Father of the Lord Jesus who cared for his little children.

The next day John arrived in school dressed in his new suit. When Mr Smith told him how good he looked, John replied that God had given him the clothing while his father was conducting family worship.

Mr Smith laughed and replied, 'John, whenever you need anything after this just tell your father to "tak' the Book" and God will answer your prayers.' Many years later John found out that it was Mr Smith who had delivered the gift of clothing to their home.

something to think about

1. During the sermon John and his brothers and sisters took notes. At home Dad would often them ask questions to make sure they had all understood the sermon. Do you think this is a good idea? Perhaps you may want to try it.

2. Think how the Lord's Day (or Sunday) is a special day? It should be the most enjoyable day of the week. Make sure you never think of it as being boring.
   Read Exodus 20:8. Here it tells us to keep the Sabbath Day holy (holy means 'set apart'). How do you think Sunday can be both enjoyable and holy?

3. Try and read a modern version of 'Pilgrim's Progress' by John Bunyan. When my brother and I were young my mother read 'Pilgrims Progress' to us when we went to bed. It took a long time but we enjoyed the story.

4
School days

Until he was almost twelve, John attended the village school where all the children studied the same subjects. Of great importance was the study of the Scriptures and the Catechism. The children were expected to learn Bible passages and the answers to the 107 questions of the Shorter Catechism. Then came the study of English grammar, history and geography. For those hoping to attend University, it was necessary to study mathematics, Latin and Greek.

One year John gained the top mark in the Latin examination and as prizes were awarded annually for excellence, he expected to be given the prize he had won. However, John was very disappointed when the son of a wealthy family received the honour. He gradually realised that Mr Smith was unfair in awarding the school prizes. The children of well-to-do families usually received all the praise and prizes whether they deserved it or not. John began to wonder if all of his studies were worth the effort.

When John was almost twelve he refused to attend Mr Smith's school any more as one day the teacher grabbed him and in a fit of anger, gave him a severe belting. John ran home from school and told his mother he would never go back again. When she pleaded with him to return and continue with his studies, John turned around and went back to Mr Smith, who, when he saw John again, attacked him, this time kicking him as well. For John that was 'the straw that broke the camel's back'!

He turned and ran home, telling his parents he would never again return to Mr Smith's school.

Later Mr Smith visited the Paton home and despite his apologies and pleading for him to return to his school, John refused. However, John knew the value of education and realised that if he was to serve the Lord one day as a minister or missionary, he would have to do more studies. But there was no other school for John to attend and as he was not going to allow Mr Smith to knock him about, it meant starting work.

John's father employed him in his stocking factory, where, like the other employees, he worked from six o'clock in the morning until ten o'clock at night. This was a long working day, but the weavers had an hour break for lunch and half an hour for both breakfast and tea. In his spare time John studied his books, especially Greek and Latin which were necessary for anyone planning to enter the ministry.

As John worked hard weaving stockings he wondered how he would ever be able to serve the Lord on the mission field. Little did he know that his work at the stocking loom was good preparation for his work amongst the cannibals of the New Hebrides.

During those difficult days, he prayed that God would open the way for him to enter the ministry. His parents also prayed that their first-born son would one day become a missionary, taking the gospel to the heathen people in the South Seas.

John continued to discover that his God was the God of the impossible, the God who answered the prayers of his believing people. Early in his life John learned that he could trust God and that he would not be disappointed.

One year, the potato crops had failed, and most farmers and families found that their vegetable gardens didn't produce much food. John's father was away in Hawick selling stockings from his small factory while his mother was left to care for the children. John's father expected to return with sufficient money to buy the expensive food available in the shops. However, the flour barrel was empty, there were no potatoes in the bag, and the cupboard was bare. That night there was no food on the table for the family and everyone went to bed hungry, the youngest ones crying.

Before going to bed, their mother gathered the children about her and prayed to God that he might give them food for the table. That night while the children slept, their mother pleaded with God to somehow provide food for the family. She fell asleep, trusting that God would give them what they needed – plates of food on the breakfast table. She trusted her heavenly Father, who cared for the little sparrows, to take care of the needs of his children.

Early the next day mother was up and about before the children awoke. She set the table even though there was no food to be eaten; but she trusted that God would provide the food they needed.

She heard the carrier stop outside their front door. Then there was a knock, and to mother's surprise the carrier told her that he had some parcels for her from John's grandfather who lived in Lockerbie. He knew that food was in short supply and as he had plenty he had sent them a bag of potatoes, a sack of flour and some freshly made cheese.

God knew that they needed food and even before John's mother had prayed, the Lord had told the old man to send the packages. Quickly mother woke the family and with them all kneeling she thanked God for his faithfulness in answering her prayers. She knew that there was now sufficient food in the larder until well after their father had returned.

John's mother then said to her children, 'O my children, love your Heavenly Father, tell him in faith and prayer all your needs and he will supply your wants so far as it shall be for your good and his glory.' That morning everyone sat down to a full plate of food. John now knew that the God he loved cared for his children.

something to think about

1. What did John find unfair at school at the end of the school year?

2. What was John hoping and praying to be when he became a man?

3. What did John learn about God and prayer in his young days?
   Read 1 Kings 17:7-16. How does this compare with what happened in John's family?

5
Work commences

As John wanted to further his education he saved all the money he could while working with his father. After some time he had saved sufficient to meet the costs involved in attending the Dumfries' Academy for six weeks. This secondary education stirred John's desire to return to full time studies. As he didn't have enough money he set about finding a well paid job.

Soon he had work with a Government department that was surveying Scotland. The pay was good and the hours of work much shorter than when he worked at his father's stocking making factory. John had to walk four miles each way to work, which started at 9:00 am and finished at 4:00pm.

During his lunch hour, instead of playing football with his work mates, he found a quiet place where he read his books. One of the overseers, seeing John alone and reading, called him into his office and asked him what he was studying. John replied truthfully that his great hope was to serve the Lord as a minister of the gospel.

Soon after that meeting he was called before the work officials, who offered him some special training in Woolwich at the Government's expense, and a promotion when his special studies were completed. If John accepted the work offer, he would be obliged to sign a contract to work in the position for seven years.

John thanked them for their kind offer, but said that he would agree to a contract to work for three or four years, but not for seven years.

The senior official was surprised with John's answer and asked, 'Why? Will you refuse an offer that many gentlemen's sons would be proud of?'

John replied, 'My life is given to another Master, so I cannot bind myself to this work for seven years.'

Sharply the official demanded, 'To whom?'

'To the Lord Jesus,' John replied, 'and I want to prepare as soon as possible for his service in the proclaiming of the gospel.'

A furious paymaster demanded, 'Accept my offer, or you are dismissed on the spot!'

John replied, 'I am extremely sorry if you do so, but to bind myself for seven years would probably frustrate the purpose of my life; and though I am greatly obliged to you, I cannot enter such an agreement.'

With that John was dismissed from the work, collected his pay, and left his work mates. When the Rector of the Dumfries Academy heard what had happened he told John he could return to his studies for as long as he wanted – and he would not be required to pay any fees. This was a welcome offer, but John could not take it up as he needed money to support himself. He knew that he couldn't expect his father to pay his expenses, as he had a large family for which to care.

He knew he needed another job so went to the Lamb Fair at Lockerbie where he was asked by a farmer to bind a sheaf. John had never done that type of work, with the result that his sheaf fell apart as soon as the farmer grabbed it by the binding. The kind farmer then showed John how to bind a sheaf. His second sheaf didn't fall apart when it was picked up and shaken. The farmer picked up his third sheaf, and threw it across the field. When it held together he shouted out, 'Right now, my lad; go ahead!'

John now had work on the farm, but when the farmer's wife saw him she decided that he should sleep at the house in her son's bedroom and not with the tough farm hands whose beds were made up in the hayloft. In his spare time John prepared a garden in front of the farmhouse, where he grew vegetables and flowers. All of this proved useful when he was on the mission field.

When the casual work came to an end, John was paid his wages and given a present.

John applied for work in Glasgow with the West Campbell Street Reformed Presbyterian Church, who wanted a young man to work amongst families. This job involved visiting families who once attended the church. The work also involved the distribution of tracts. This work suited John as the pay was £50 a year and one year's training in a college which would qualify him to become a schoolteacher.

It was time to move to Glasgow and be interviewed for the work with the Glasgow congregation of the church to which the Paton family belonged.

John wrapped his few belongings in a parcel and set out for Glasgow. This meant a forty-mile walk to the railway, where he'd catch a train for Glasgow. John's father walked several miles with his eldest son, and when the time came for farewells, he prayed for John, that God would watch over him. Then taking his son by the hand, and with tears in his eyes he said, 'God bless you, my son! Your father's God prosper you and keep you from all evil!'

When his father hugged John he knew it was time to part. John turned and ran. Walking along he promised God that he would always 'live and act so as never to grieve or dishonour such a father and mother as he [God] had given me.'

The Paton family was very close to each other and parting was difficult. In fact when he was much older he said of the children that they 'stuck to each other and the old folks like burs.'

something to think about

1. John was told to sign a contract to work for seven years or else be dismissed from his job. He said that he wanted to serve the Lord Jesus. This made him very unpopular. Do you think that Christians are still unpopular today?
See Matthew 10:34-38; John 15:18-23.

2. John promised God he would never bring shame upon his family. That is a wonderful promise to make. How can young people bring shame upon their parents and the church? Eli was ashamed of his sons.
Read about them in 1 Samuel 2:12-26.

3. John went to work on a farm. What did he do there? How do you think this helped him to prepare for the mission field?

6
Life in the big city

Attending the interview, John discovered that there was a second person to be interviewed. The result was that the work was to be shared between them, and they were to share the £50 wages.

The two young men became good friends, but the long hours of work and little good food resulted in them both becoming ill. After visiting a doctor, John was ordered home for a time of rest, good food and fresh air. His mother and Father were pleased to have their son home with them and it wasn't long before his health had greatly improved.

John then took a teaching job in a small school at Girvan. After saving £10 he resigned and returned to Glasgow. Before long his money was almost used and he began to think he should sell his books in order to survive until he found work. However, he saw a notice in a window asking for a teacher at Maryhill Free Church School.

Seeing a bus going in the right direction and having the fare, John hopped on, thanking God for guiding him through the streets to see the advertisement in the window. Following an interview, he was soon standing before a class, only this time the students were young men and women from a rather tough area of Glasgow. The three previous teachers left the school because of the terrible behaviour in the classroom.

The minister came to John and placing a thick, heavy cane on the table said, 'Use that freely or you will never keep order here!' Putting it aside, John replied, 'That will be my last resort.'

The night classes consisted of tough young men and women who worked in the mills and coal mines. Most of these students had little respect for schoolteachers and when the opportunity presented itself they behaved terribly. Everyone laughed and talked and one couple caused so much noise that when John ordered them to be quiet the young man jumped to his feet and put up his fists ready to fight.

John knew that he had to control this man or his teaching career was at an end. Locking the school door he warned the students to remain seated while he dealt with the outrageous behaviour. Picking up his cane he hit the man who tried to punch him. For some time John hit the man with the cane while he tried to dodged the blows. After a few minutes the young student had taken enough punishment. He sat down in his seat while the class sat in quietness. John quietly said that he didn't want to use the cane but would do so again if necessary.

Soon thereafter John was able to put the cane away and the class worked well.

John's reputation spread throughout the city as a sound teacher who kept control in the classroom. This meant that more students transferred to the school. However, as the school was doing so well, the school committee decided to employ a teacher with higher qualifications.

Soon John would be out of work and looking for a job. Again he took his need to God and was sure that his prayer would be answered in such a way that God would be glorified.

The night before John was to leave Maryhill School he received a letter from the Glasgow City Mission asking him to appear before the committee responsible for selecting someone for missionary work in the city.

John's knowledge of the Bible was questioned and he was taken to some poor families where he spoke to them about the

Lord Jesus. The selection committee wanted to see how John got on with people. He also preached a sermon before a congregation, and the examiners.

He had little time to prepare his sermon, but the Lord took care of him and all went well. Several days later John was employed as one of the city's missionaries.

John's reputation spread throughout the city as a sound teacher who kept control in the classroom.

something to think about

1. John left home for life in the city. In what way was he different to the 'Prodigal (or Lost) Son'? **It will help you to answer the question if you read the story in Luke 15:11-32.**

2. When John needed help what was the first thing he always did? What do we learn from that?

3. Why is it important to know your Bible and to read it carefully?
   See Acts 17:10-12; 2 Timothy 3:14-17.

7
Preparations for the overseas mission field

At the Glasgow City Mission John's day was filled with work. Four hours each day, Monday to Saturday, he was to visit homes conducting Bible studies and prayer meetings wherever he could. Some meetings were held after tea. On the Lord's Day a special evangelistic service was held in a hayloft over a shed where cows were kept. To get onto the hayloft the congregation had to climb a steep wooden stairway outside the building.

The work didn't produce many results, but when the suggestion came that John should be moved to another section of the city if numbers did not increase, the congregation set to work inviting their friends to attend the meetings.

John gathered about him a group of helpers and soon new prayer meetings and Bible Study groups were formed. To these were added Psalm singing classes and communicant classes for those who wanted church membership.

Sundays started with a 7.00 am Bible class. John used to run from house to house, waking people in time to attend their classes. Soon almost one hundred people attended the Bible studies. When people were converted they began to take care of their tidiness. They dressed in better clothes than before, and many started wearing shoes to the classes and worship.

As the numbers attending the Bible Study grew the church purchased some new buildings. No longer was the hayloft used.

One building was used as a church and another as a school for the poor. A teacher was employed and John's people helped with books, clothes and food for the children attending.

Despite the additional workload John was expected to still give at least four hours daily to home visitation. Frequently he was assisted by the young members of the congregation, who were always ready to hand out tracts and speak to people about the Lord Jesus Christ, the Saviour.

When John heard that someone was sick and in need of assistance, he visited the home himself.

There was widespread drunkenness in the area which resulted in much crime and broken homes. John believed in 'total abstinence', and did all he could to encourage people to give up drinking alcohol altogether. In one home where Bible study was held, the Irish wife was married to an alcoholic husband, whose drinking caused much unhappiness. He spent his wages before any food was bought for his family and often hit his wife with a belt in his drunken rage.

Over time he heard the Bible studies in his house. The Holy Spirit showed him what a wicked sinner he was; he had broken God's holy laws! He repented of his sins and turned to Christ for his salvation. He gave up drinking alcohol. Knowing what damage strong drink was doing to families, he began inviting drunkards to the Bible studies and prayer meetings.

Often John preached the gospel in the open air where he urged drunkards to turn to Christ in faith. He forcefully told them they could overcome the power that alcohol had over them by looking to God in true repentance. As drunkards were saved and refused to spend their money in the hotels, the publicans decided John's preaching had to be stopped – they were losing money!

A group of hoteliers decided to act. They tried to get the police to prevent the public gatherings. The Officer-in-Charge agreed to send some officers to John's meetings to make sure there was no trouble.

When outsiders heard of this, crowds came along expecting to see a riot, but this was not to happen. One police officer stood beside John, while some of his men mixed with the large crowd. They joined in with the singing of hymns and psalms, and those who had come along to break up John's gathering, found themselves forced to stay and listen to the gospel message.

Many of the police supported John's work as converted drunkards no longer gave them trouble. The publicans, however, were furious. One group dragged a cart across the entrance to a church where John was to speak. When some of his friends attempted to move it, they were arrested and taken to the police station.

John ran after the police, and reaching the police station found that the constables on duty that day supported the publicans. They refused to listen to John's complaints and were ready to charge the men with breaking the law.

Suddenly there appeared a well-dressed gentleman who offered to pay the bail needed to have the men released. A short discussion was held with the constables and the man announced, 'I know the whole case, I will expose it to the bottom; expect me here to stand by the missionary and these young men on Monday morning!'

Before John could thank the man he had walked out of the police station. The police came to John and politely told him that the charges were withdrawn and all were free to go. God had watched over his servant!

On one occasion John was asked to visit a young doctor who was a drunkard. His young wife and two little children were very unhappy. The doctor planned to kill himself because of the hurt his drunken behaviour was causing them.

John began visiting him, once, sometimes twice a day. Again when he decided to kill himself, John came into his bedroom.

'Put all these people out of the room,' the doctor begged. 'I will be quiet. I will do everything you ask!'

When everyone had left the bedroom, John sat down beside him and asked, 'If you had a Bible here we might read a chapter, taking turns, a verse each.'

The doctor looked at John and said, 'There was once a Bible above the press over there. If you can climb up it might still be there.'

John found the Bible and placing it on a small table both he and the doctor sat down. After reading a chapter John asked, 'Now, shall we pray?'

To this the doctor replied, 'Yes,'

'You pray first,' John suggested, but the doctor replied, 'I curse, I cannot pray; would you have me curse God to his face?'

John replied, 'You promised to do all that I asked; you must pray, or try to pray, and don't let me hear that you cannot.'

The doctor answered, 'I cannot curse God on my knees; let me stand, and I will curse him; I cannot pray.'

John, gently holding his shoulders so he remained kneeling, asked, 'Just try to pray, and don't let me hear that you cannot.'

'O Lord, you know I cannot pray,' he said, trying to stand up. John then took over and completed the man's prayer, praying as if he were the drunkard before him.

John then told the man that he had to collect his books and get to College for the day's lessons. However, before he left he asked the doctor to lie down and have a sleep. He promised to sit by his bedside until he fell asleep.

After John's lessons were finished he returned to be met by a smiling doctor who threw his arms about him and said, 'Thank God, I can pray now! I awoke today from my sleep and for the first time in my life prayed with my wife and children. Now I shall do so every day and serve God while I live. God has had such great mercy upon me!'

Not every person John met repented of his sins. John was asked to visit a man who was dying. His wife was a Roman Catholic who wanted John to come and would not have the priest. John spent much time with the man, who, when he mentioned the name of Jesus, shouted, 'Pray to the devil for me!'

The ungodly man continued, 'Yes, I believe there is a devil, and a God, and a just God too; but I have hated him in life and

I hate him in death.' And with that terrible confession he passed into eternity, to face God!

John also met true Christians who were dying. One was an eight year old boy who repeated the words,

I lay my sins on Jesus
The spotless Lamb of God.

Looking at his weeping parents he said, 'I am going to soon be with Jesus; but I sometimes fear that I may not see you there.'

'Why so my child?' his mother asked.

'Because, ' he answered, 'if you were on your way to heaven and seeing Jesus there, you would pray about it, and sing about it; you would talk about Jesus to others and tell them of that happy meeting with him in glory. All this my dear Sunday school teacher taught me and she will meet me there. Now why didn't you, my father and mother, tell me all those things about Jesus, if you are going to meet him too?'

John also had dealings with some of the Roman Catholics in the area. Many wrote hateful letters to him while others threw stones and boiling water over him as he walked along the street. Some of the priests even cursed him from the pulpits of their churches.

John had been working for several years as a missionary to the local people. He was elected an elder of the church and continued with his work, knowing that is was all good training for the foreign mission field.

In all he spent ten years serving the Lord Jesus in Glasgow. He saw many people converted. During his time there he studied at the University of Glasgow and the Reformed Presbyterian Church Hall. He also spent time studying medicine, knowing that one day he would be able to use all of his God-given skills serving the Lord Jesus Christ on the mission field.

something to think about

1. John met many people who were often drunk. He believed in 'total abstinence'. Do you know what this means?
   Galatians 5:19-21 says that people who do certain things will not inherit the kingdom of God. Are you surprised to see drunkenness on the list?

2. Why was the dying boy so upset with his parents? Was this the same way that John's parents had brought him up?

3. John spent ten years in Glasgow preparing for the mission field. Why do you think he needed all this long time?

8
Time to leave for the New Hebrides

John enjoyed his work in Glasgow but all the time he felt God's call to the overseas mission fields. As he carried out his duties, his mind continued to think about the heathen men and women going into a lost eternity, because they had no knowledge of the Lord Jesus.

One day, the Rev John Inglis, a missionary supported by his church, was home on leave. Much of his time was spent travelling about, giving talks about the mission work in the New Hebrides and appealing for new labourers to give themselves for this work. However, no one offered themselves for that dangerous, but important activity.

John attended the annual meeting of the Synod of the Reformed Presbyterian Church of Scotland where the call was made for volunteers for mission work in the New Hebrides. When no one offered their services, the delegates were each given a sheet of paper and invited to write the names of three men who, in their opinion, would be suitable mission workers.

John waited quietly as names were counted but no person's name appeared on all sheets. When this was announced to the Synod, John felt like jumping to his feet and calling out, 'Here am I! Send me!'

To be sure of God's call to the work, he went home and prayed about the matter. Several days later he approached the Missions Committee of his church and offered himself as a missionary for the New Hebrides. John was readily accepted

by the committee. When he returned home and told his friend
and fellow student, Joseph Copeland, what he had done, Joseph
made up his mind that he also would apply for work in the New
Hebrides.

Both men were accepted by the Committee, subject to their
passing the examination that ministers of the gospel were
required to pass. They were also to undertake a study of medicine and other skills, as they would not be close to help when
they were working in their particular area.

When John told his delighted parents of his decision they
were overjoyed. They told him that on the day of his birth they
had given him back to the Lord, and from that day forward
had prayed that the day would come when he became a
missionary on some foreign field.

Many of the people with whom he had been working for
many years, begged him not to throw away his life in some far
distant land. They reminded John that Glasgow was a mission
field and that his work there was being blessed by God. John
took little notice of these words because he had not seen any
real concern shown by them for sinners at home or abroad. In
fact he knew that many spent more on themselves than they
gave to support the work of missions.

One old Christian tried to discourage him by saying to him,
'The cannibals! You'll be eaten by cannibals!' John reminded
the man that he was aged and would soon die and be laid in a
grave where his body would be eaten by the worms. John went
on to say, 'If I can but live and die serving and honouring the
Lord Jesus, it will make no difference to me whether I am eaten
by cannibals or by worms. On the great day, my resurrection
body will rise as fair as yours, in the likeness of our risen
Redeemer.'

The old man stood up and waving his hands in the air left
John with the words, 'After that I have nothing to say!'

John left the day of his death, and his manner of dying, firmly in the hands of God. He'd risked his life often in Glasgow when he visited the homes of people suffering from cholera, and other deadly diseases.

John was concerned about the work he had been doing in Glasgow. He didn't want it to fall apart, but when his brother Walter gave up his well paid job and accepted John's position, he knew all would be well.

John used some of his savings to pay his family's debts and prepared for his departure with his friend Joseph.

Both men passed their examinations and were licensed to preach the gospel on 1 December 1857. John and Joseph then spent four months travelling throughout Scotland, speaking about the work they were to undertake and seeking prayer and support while they were overseas.

On 23 March 1858 both men were ordained as ministers of the gospel and set apart as missionaries to the New Hebrides. John's friends in Glasgow set to work making dresses, kilts and trousers for John and Joseph to take with them. They would be used by the missionaries and the people amongst whom they worked. The members of John's Bible classes continued to send packages of clothing for many years. Whenever a parcel arrived John remembered the faces of those who had made the clothing.

The time had arrived for John, his new bride Mary, and Joseph to board their ship and commence the long journey to the New Hebrides.

something to think about

1. Where is the New Hebrides and what is it called today?
    There are maps in this book but also have a look in your
    atlas.

2. John was not afraid to die. **Read Psalm 23**
    What had happened to him in Glasgow to teach him that
    his death, and his life, were entirely in the Lord's hands?

3. Why were John's parents so delighted in John's decision to
    go to the New Hebrides? Was this an answer to their
    prayers?

9
The New Hebrides at last

It was on 16 April 1858 that the Clutha sailed from the port of Greenock, bound for Australia, the 'Land Down Under'. This was the first stage of their long journey to the New Hebrides. The three, John, Mary and Joseph, stood together on the ship's deck and watched Scotland's shoreline gradually disappear.

John had married a godly young woman, Mary Ann Robson. She was well educated in an age when girls received very little schooling. Like John she wanted to serve the Lord on the mission field, and was overjoyed that she and her husband would soon be on one of the islands in the New Hebrides.

The long journey passed without any difficulty and John and Joseph were allowed to conduct worship services and Bible Studies with the crew and passengers.

When the ship docked at Melbourne, John and Mary went ashore to spend several days with some local missionaries. Joseph, however, agreed to remain on board and take care of their luggage and two small boats they were taking with them to the New Hebrides. He also made enquiries about boats that were sailing to their mission islands.

Soon he had made arrangements for their passage on the American ship, the 'Francis P. Sage' which was sailing to Penang. The captain agreed to drop them off at Aneityum, an island in the southern section of the New Hebrides. The trip took twelve days and this journey was more rowdy than the trip to Australia. There was a lot of shouting and swearing by the second mate and the crew. The captain said he employed the second mate to keep the crew working – he could both swear at the men and knock them about if necessary.

When Aneityum came in view, the captain dropped anchor about ten miles off the coast and refused to take the ship any closer to land. He feared that the crew would desert the ship because of their harsh treatment by the second mate.

At last a boat arrived from the island and they were asked what they wanted. When it was realised that there were three missionaries on board, the small boat returned to the island with the news. The missionaries already working on the island sent out two small boats – the 'John Knox' and the 'Colombia'.

When they reached the ship, the cargo was transferred and John and Mary, and two local missionaries, found themselves perched up like four sea birds on top of the cargo on the 'John Knox'. As the boats began to move apart, a crane became entangled, breaking off the mast. John pulled Mary away from the tangled crane and ropes, and it was only his quick action that prevented her being killed. Eventually, rowing hard, the crew of the 'Colombia' made it safely to the island with the 'John Knox' in tow.

It was on 30 August 1858 that Joseph, John and Mary stepped onto the soil of the New Hebrides, having left Scotland four and a half months earlier.

For some weeks John and Joseph assisted the missionaries with some buildings, while Mary spent time with the ladies, learning about life on the islands.

At last it was time to take up their permanent work. John and Mary were to work on the island of Tanna, at Port Resolution, where a Mr and Mrs Mathieson lived on the southern side. Joseph was to spend his time giving help to John and the Mathiesons. He had the use of the 'John Knox' to carry building materials and other useful goods to the two mission fields on Tanna.

The first step was to purchase land from the tribal chief. Payment was made with axes, knives, fishhooks, blankets and clothes. However, before building commenced the chiefs then demanded extra payment before they allowed any trees to be cut down. When it came time to build a fence, the chiefs refused permission, unless extra payments were made. The demand was plainly put: 'Cut down a tree before payment is made and you will die!'

Then came the bargaining for permission to burn lime in kilns, to make plaster for the walls of the buildings. There was little difficulty getting the sugar cane leaves to make thatched roofs.

The missionaries made a mistake when they bought land close to the ocean. The air was very moist and was home to the malaria carrying mosquitoes which bred in the many water pools. Disease was always a present companion of the missionaries. Much later one of the chiefs told John, 'Missi, if you stay here, you will soon die! No Tanna-man sleeps so low down as you do in this damp weather or he too would die. We sleep on the high ground, and the trade-wind keeps us well...'

It was there, in a sheltered spot close to the shore of a lovely bay, and surrounded by palm trees, that John and Mary built their first home and commenced work amongst the natives, who were described by a sailor as 'the ugliest, the most indecent, the most grotesque, and the most utterly barbarous both in appearance and actual fact, of any people whom we have yet seen.'

John and Mary had come to present these people with the gospel of salvation through faith in Christ.

something to think about

1. Why do you think Australia was (and still often is) called the 'Land Down Under'?

2. Did the people of Tanna think the missionaries were sensible in buying land near the sea?

3. One of the boats was named 'John Knox'. There was a man named John Knox who lived about 500 years ago; see if you can find out who he was.

4. The captain was afraid that the crew would desert the ship because of the harsh and unkind way the second mate had treated them.
    In 1 Thessalonians 5:15 Paul tells us how we should act towards each other. What does he say?

10
Meeting the cannibals

Leaving Mary behind John, with other missionaries, arrived on Tanna to build a home. His first sight of the local natives horrified him. The men were naked with brightly painted faces. Some would have a red cheek on one side of their face and black on the other side. Many had their eyebrows painted white and the chin painted a different colour. In their matted hair they had feathers which stuck out at different angles. Wherever they went they carried a weapon – axe, spear or club. They were ready to fight at a moment's notice. The women only wore grass skirts with necklaces and earrings made from shells.

John even wondered if he should have stayed in Scotland and served the Lord in Glasgow. However, he knew that these poor natives urgently needed the gospel of salvation. Only twenty years before the first protestant missionaries, John Williams and James Harris, had landed on Tanna. No sooner had they set foot on the island than they were clubbed to death and cooked for lunch by the local natives.

George Turner and Henry Nisbet arrived soon after but they were forced to escape at night in a small boat. The natives intended making a meal of them. A whaling ship rescued them and they moved to Samoa where they worked amongst the natives.

In 1848 Dr John Geddie and his wife settled on Aneityum. They were joined by Dr John Inglis and his wife, who commenced a work on the other side of the island. Their labours were greatly blessed by God and 3,500 natives threw away their carved idols and trusted their salvation to the Lord Jesus. Joseph Copeland undertook the translation of the Bible into their native language and assisted the natives pay for their Bibles with crops of arrowroot which sold for good prices in Great Britain.

John was to be witness to many wars between the native tribes on Tanna. The local tribe promised to take care of him but their chief said they could not protect him from the inland tribes. A fight broke out and John was fearful when he heard blood curdling cries and shouts. Occasionally he heard gunfire.

Later he heard that five or six warriors had been killed. Their bodies were taken to a spot several miles from John's home and there beside a spring of water, cooked and eaten. The next morning when a young native companion from Aneityum returned with an empty water can, he told John, 'Missi, this is a dark land. The people of this land do dark works. At the boiling spring they have cooked and feasted upon the slain. They have washed the blood into the water; they have bathed there, polluting everything. I cannot get pure water to make your tea. What shall I do?'

Sad to say, the young native was more concerned about the polluted water than the men who had been killed, cooked and eaten. Dr Inglis told the boy they would drink coconut milk that day.

During night the air was filled with much shouting and loud screams, and when the missionaries asked what was happening they were told that the wives of their dead warriors had been killed and with their husband's bodies were buried out to sea. They believed that this meant the spirits of the wives would be able to serve their husbands in the land beyond this world.

As the missionaries continued their building a native picked up a building tool and said, 'Nungsi nari enu?'

John guessed he was saying, 'What is this?'

John then held out a piece of wood and asked, 'Nungsi nari enu?' Soon John and the natives began to learn the different languages.

When Mary joined John on Tanna on 5 November 1858 she wrote to her parents saying, 'I have never seen such a lovely spot'. However, soon after the birth of their first child, a son (born 12 February 1859) whom they named Peter, Mary fell ill and died on 3 March 1859. Before she died she confessed to Joseph Conrad, 'You must not think that I regret coming here. If I had the same thing to do over again I would do it. I do not regret leaving home and friends.'

John dug his wife's grave and laid her to rest, waiting for the day when the Lord Jesus would return and Mary would be raised in her new body. A couple of weeks later little Peter died and John laid his body to rest beside that of his mother. He decorated the grave with pieces of white coral.

John was greatly saddened but could only say, 'My God and my Father is too wise and loving to make any mistakes in what he does.' Often he came to the grave and there prayed that God would bless his work and bring the warring natives of Tanna to faith in Christ.

something to think about

1. How did John cope with the death of his wife Mary and son Peter? **Read Job 34:12.** Think what both Job and John say about God never making mistakes. Why do you think this is true?

2. What law of God was being broken by the cannibals? **Read Exodus 20:13**

3. There was a lot of fighting between the tribes on Tanna. What is Jesus teaching us in **Matthew 5:21-22?** Why is it important to avoid being angry with other people?

11
A dangerous life on Tanna

The natives of Tanna were very religious. They worshipped the spirits of their dead relatives and warriors. They feared their gods of stone and word and frequently sacrificed people in an effort to keep them happy. The village sacred man claimed that he could put a curse on anyone. All he needed was something the person had touched and after making the curse, expected the cursed one to die. They also claimed to control the weather, life, death, health, sickness, war and peace.

The natives wanted nothing to do with John's God and the sinners' Saviour, Jesus Christ. Often they blamed John and Jehovah for everything terrible that happened. When an old chief Nowhat left Tanna for his home, he fell ill and died. Nowhat's brother returned to Tanna and accused John of being responsible for Nowhat's death. Soon the brother fell ill and the natives blamed John's God for that sickness also.

A meeting was held where several tribes decided to kill John. Some women had been killed, cooked and eaten as a sacrifice to the tribal god, but a local chieftain jumped to his feet and waving his club about him said, 'The man that kills Missi[1] must first kill me and my people. We shall stand by them and defend them till death!' John and his companions gave thanks to God for using the local chief to protect him.

On another occasion during a long drought, John and his God were blamed. The chiefs had met and decided to drive all the missionaries from the island. This time chief Nouka and his nephew, Miaki the war-chief, visited John and asked him to pray to his God for rain or there would be nothing they could do to prevent him being killed. John prayed for rain, which began to fall the following Lord's Day. However, the rain turned into a storm which damaged the fruit trees and caused much sickness among the natives. Again John and his God were blamed for the island's trouble.

Often the missionaries were blamed for troubles caused by white traders who cheated the islanders out of their goods. They sold guns and bullets to the natives, which only helped the killing during times of war. When three traders were murdered on the island of Erromanga, some of the natives of Tanna decided to kill any white men on the island, including the missionaries. During the drinking party that followed, some warriors from an inland tribe crept in and slaughtered some sleeping warriors. Now the threat of war hung over the tribes.

Early in life, little boys were taught how to use their weapons to kill other people. The adult men spent their time resting and feasting when not fighting. It was the women who worked the garden and did all the heavy work. They were slaves to the men who treated them very cruelly. On one occasion when John was trying to prevent this wicked behaviour a chief said, 'If we did not beat our women they would never work; they would not fear and obey us but when we have belted and killed and feasted on two or three, the rest are all very quiet and good for a long time.'

John encouraged the men to show kindness to their wives telling them that this would make them happier and encourage them to work even better. When some Christian natives visited the island with their wives, they showed the local natives how to treat their wives with kindness. One chief told John he wanted to treat his wife better but could not as the tribe would laugh at him.

And all the time John told the natives of the salvation that was to be found in the Lord Jesus Christ. He told them about sin and death, heaven and hell, and then told them of the heaven that was theirs through faith in Christ.

---

something to think about

1. Being religious does not always mean that people worship
   the true God. What did the people on Tanna use to make
   their gods and how did they often try to keep them happy?
   Read Exodus 20:3. What does the true God say about
   worshipping any other gods?

2. What were the native boys of Tanna taught and why was
   this wrong? We have already looked at this in a previous
   chapter?

3. What was John trying to teach the natives?
   Read Ephesians 5:25. Stated here is the reason why this
   should happen. What is it?

12
You shall not steal!

John soon discovered that the natives were thieves. The only thing they believed wrong with theft was being caught in the act. When he caught someone in the act of stealing his property, and demanded that it be given to him, the thief usually started waving his big club about and John lost his possession.

Often when John was talking to one of the natives who saw something on the floor that they wanted, they gradually put their foot on it and grabbed it with their toes. They would walk out of the house with the item under their foot.

One day after putting his washing on the clothes line, John left the wives of two native Christian missionaries to keep guard. However, when the war-chief, Miaki appeared, he grabbed John by the arm and pulled him into the house saying, 'Missi, come in, quick, quick! I want to tell you something and get your advice!' A few moments later John heard his women guards calling out, 'Missi, Missi, come quick. Miaki's men are stealing your sheets and blankets!'

Of course Miaki denied that any of his men would do such a terrible thing and as he smashed his club into the bushes about him promised John, 'This is how I will smash these fellows, and make them return your clothes!' However, Miaki made no effort to get John's possessions and return them.

Over time the natives stole his fowls, goats, cooking utensils and kettle. John offered a towel to the one who returned his possessions, especially his kettle. All he could do was take his problem to the Lord, knowing that all theft would end when the natives turned to the living God in faith. John found the going difficult, especially when his friend Joseph Copeland, left for another mission station.

One morning John was met by several very excited natives, who shouted out, 'Missi, Missi, there is a god or a ship on fire, or something of fear coming over the sea! We see no flames but it smokes like a volcano. Is it a spirit, a god, or a ship on fire? What is it? What is it?'

John, knowing that it was a ship, decided that now he might have some of his property returned.

'I cannot go at once,' he replied. 'I must first dress in my best clothes; it will likely be one of Queen Victoria's men-of-war, coming to ask me if your conduct is good or bad – whether you are stealing my property, or threatening my life, or how you are treating me.'

Then two chiefs appeared and asked, 'Missi, will it be a ship of war?'

John refused to go and look, but replied, 'I think it will.'

The worried chiefs then asked, 'Missi, only tell us, will he ask you if we have been stealing your things?'

'I expect he will,' John replied.

'And will you tell him?' the chiefs asked.

'I must tell him the truth. If he asks, I will tell him,' John replied.

'Oh, Missi, don't tell him,' came the request. 'Everything shall be brought back to you at once and no one will be allowed to steal from you again.'

'Be quick,' John told them. 'Everything must be returned before he comes.'

At once the natives disappeared and soon John's stolen property began to appear, even the stolen kettle. However, a quick look showed that the lid of the kettle was missing. 'I don't see the lid of the kettle here yet,' John pointed out.

'No,' replied one of the chiefs. 'It is on the other side of the island and will be here tomorrow.'

John ordered the three fearful chiefs, Nauka, Miaki and Nowar to remain with him and meet the commander of the ship. Captain Vernon of HMS Cordelia, a steam driven ship, had heard of the ill treatment of the missionaries and decided to visit the island and frighten the natives. Dressed in his full uniform and accompanied by some armed sailors, Captain Vernon came ashore to meet the three chiefs who had tried to dress in their best clothing. All it did was make them look silly.

The war-chief Miaki, feeling brave, asked, 'Missi, this great chief whom Queen Victoria, has sent to visit you in her man-of-war, cannot go over the whole island to be seen by all our people. I wish you to ask him if he will stand by a tree, and allow me to put a spear on the ground at his heel, and make a nick in it at the height of his head. The spear will be sent around the island to show the people how tall he is.'

Captain Vernon was happy to oblige, but as he wanted to frighten the natives he invited the chiefs and other warriors to came aboard the ship the next day.

The next day the natives appeared, carrying their weapons. However, Captain Vernon warned them against harming the missionaries or any Englishman. Then he took the group on board to see the firing of the guns. The first shell was fired out to sea and the natives began to show some nervousness. Then the Captain gave the order to fire a shot onto the land. This time the shot tore through the trees in the coconut grove, breaking off branches and terrifying the natives who asked to be allowed to return to the shore. For many years the natives told the story of 'the great fire god of the sea and the Captain of the great white Queen who visited our island.'

something to think about

1. What commandment did the natives break?
   Read Exodus 20:15. There are many ways we can break
   that commandment – even taking small things that don't
   belong to us is stealing. We can even steal from God. How
   do you think we can do that?

2. Why were the natives of Tanna afraid of Queen Victoria?

3. Why did Captain Vernon frighten the natives?

13
Troublesome times

It wasn't long before another ship called at Tanna to buy coconuts, fresh fruit and other foods. This was a whaling ship, the 'Camden Packet'. Captain Allan was a Christian who treated the local natives fairly. While there several of the crew repaired the mission boat which had been damaged on the reef.

All visitors to the island were not kind to the natives. A French ship, crewed by slaves and well armed, called at the island for fresh food. When they heard of John's dangers they offered to take him aboard and drop him off at Sydney. John thanked the ship's captain but refused the offer, knowing that if he left it would be difficult for any missionary to return.

John had made the very wise decision to move further up the hill. A native Christian Abraham, and his wife Nafatu, assisted John with the move to a block of land well above sea level. This time John paid for the land in front of the whole tribe. This was to prevent anyone coming along later and claiming the land. Abraham and his wife helped a sick John to his new house, and then carried John's possessions to the new building.

While this was happening a French ship called at the island to trade with the natives. Just as the ship was sailing away, John and Abraham set fire to the old house with its thatched roof. When the Captain of the French ship saw the flames and smoke billowing into the sky, he assumed that the natives had attacked the missionaries and burned John's house to the ground. Immediately he returned with armed men ready to attack the islanders.

'Where are they? Where are they? The scoundrels! I'll kill them and protect you,' he said to John. 'I shall punish them, the scoundrels!'

John caught him just in time and explained what had happened but the Captain warned the natives that if they caused any more trouble for John, he would return and burn their villages to the ground.

Other ships called at the island and the captains often cheated the natives and frequently paid for their cargo with guns and ammunition. They knew that this would keep the fighting going and assure the traders of good purchases which they could pay for with more guns and ammunition.

One trader, Captain Winchester and his native wife, decided to stay on the island bartering for fruit, pigs and poultry, which he sold to passing ships.

Miaki, the war chief had a brother named Rarip who came to John for protection when war broke out between some tribes. Miaki ordered him to take his place in the battle, but he had run away to John and said, 'Missi, I hate this fighting; it is not good to kill men. I will live with you!'

However, before long Miaki appeared and forced his brother to return with him and fight. In the opening part of the fighting he was killed. Quickly John went to Miaki's people where he found the islanders, both men and women, wailing and cutting their flesh with sharp knives.

When John offered a white sheep in which to wrap Rarip's body, the offer was accepted and he was given permission to conduct the funeral service, where the Scriptures were read, a psalm sung and prayer made to Jehovah. John longed for the day when the natives would turn to Christ for salvation.

The war continued with many deaths. However, soon the natives turned against Captain Winchester who had sold them

the guns and ammunition to use in warfare. When he pleaded with John to be allowed to stay at the Mission house, John refused. He didn't want the natives to think he was involved with the cruel trader. So fearful was the man that each night he slept with his wife in his boat, which was anchored well away from the shore. When a trading ship arrived Captain Winchester and his wife left the island.

Each Lord's Day John conducted worship but not many natives attended. When he told his congregation that he was going to the inland tribes to tell them of Jehovah and God's Son, who had died to save sinners from their sins, the coastal natives were unhappy. They didn't want John praying for the native tribes they were fighting: 'Missi, pray only for us, and your God will be strong to help us! ... You must not pray with the enemy, lest your God help them too.'

As a result John visited both coastal and inland tribes, warning them of God's anger because of their sinful ways. He begged them to live at peace with each other, but the fighting continued.

A Tannese family about 1850

something to think about

1. In this chapter who was 'Abraham'?
    In the Bible a man named Abraham was tested by God.
    Read about this in Genesis 22:1-19.

2. Why didn't the natives want John to tell the inland tribes
    about God and the Lord Jesus Christ? Of what were they
    afraid?

3. How did the natives behave when somebody died? How do
    you think Christians should behave when a friend or rela-
    tive dies? We must remember that it is not wrong to be
    sad.
    Read in John 11:35 how Jesus behaved when his friend
    died. This is also the shortest verse in the Bible.

14
Danger all around

The tribes of Tanna lived for war, killings and cannibalism. In an effort to bring a lengthy war to an end John met with twenty chiefs and pleaded with them to live at peace together. He told them the gospel and had them promise not to fight again. However, within a very short time the slaughter recommenced.

On another occasion John, Abraham and another Christian teacher, came upon some chiefs and their tribesmen who were enjoying a feast. Seeing the missionaries, some warriors came towards them with clubs raised. Even though they were unarmed John made his way to the centre of the warriors and called out, trying to make himself heard above the din: 'Fear not; I am your friend. I love you, every one of you, and am come to tell you about Jehovah God, and the way to live that pleases him.'

After conducting a short worship service everyone shook hands and the chiefs once again promised to live at peace with each other. John then gave the great chief a bright red shirt, and left fish hooks and calico to be shared among the tribes. In return John and the Christian natives were given coconuts, sugar cane and two fowls.

The coastal tribes were amazed that John and his friends had not been killed. However, the peace lasted just four weeks, and then the fighting resumed.

One morning John woke up to find his house surrounded by armed natives. He prayed what he thought might be his last earthly prayer. Then standing up he warned the warriors that God would be very displeased with them if he were killed.

After some time one of them came to him and said, 'Our conduct has been bad but now we will fight for you and kill those who hate you!' They had spared John's life, but still wanted to be involved in killing his enemies. The natives were only happy when they could fight someone.

One chief, speaking on behalf of the others, approached John and said, 'Missi, our fathers loved and worshipped the one you call the devil, the evil spirit, and we are determined to do the same, for we love the conduct of our fathers.' The chief explained that they had driven earlier missionaries from the island: 'After each of these acts, Tanna was good, we all lived like our fathers, and sickness and death left us. Now our people are determined to kill you if you do not leave the island for you are changing our customs and destroying our worship, and we hate the Jehovah worship.'

This chief had once visited Sydney, Australia, where he had seen people working on Sunday, something John said was against God's law. Surely John was wrong and those who did whatever they pleased on Sunday were right. John was able to explain to them some of the good things that come to countries when the people obey the laws of God. He then conducted a short worship service and was left in peace.

Another time a group of warriors attempted to break into his home but Clutha, his faithful dog, made such a noise that the warriors crept away. John's life was in constant danger but he trusted in the Lord to take care of him. He found comfort in Christ's words, 'Lo, I am with you always, even to the end of the age.'

Not only was John's life in danger. Namuri, one of John's Christian friends, and his wife set up house in a village and there began to teach the people of the Lord Jesus. A sacred man attacked him but John was able to nurse him back to health.

When he recovered he returned to the village to continue with his teaching.

Namuri was attacked again while he was praying. John tended his wounds but this time he could not save him. Before Namuri died he was able to speak: 'For the sake of Jesus; for the sake of Jesus. O Lord Jesus forgive them, for they do not know what they are doing. Oh, do not take away all your servants from Tanna! Do not take away your worship from this dark island. O God, bring all the Tannese people to love and follow Jesus!' This native Christian had been willing to lay down his life for the Lord Jesus whom he loved and served.

Namuri was buried near the mission house. His Christian friends wept for their loss of a good Christian companion and worker, but they all knew that the day would come when they would meet again in the presence of the Lord Jesus, whom they loved and served.

Many trading ships called at the island, causing trouble for John. One attempted to steal his small boat. When John objected the trader began to swear at him and knock him about. Many of the natives thought, 'When a white man from his own country can so pull and knock the missionary about and steal his boat and chain without being punished for it, we also may do as we please!'

Many of the sandalwood traders stole anything they could from the natives. One trader, who stored all his possessions in a cellar under his house, slept on the inside trap door that led to his belongings. The area about his house was patrolled by armed men with savage dogs.

The local natives, determined to steal his property, dug an underground passage to the cellar. While the guards and dogs patrolled the ground, the natives removed everything through the long tunnel they had dug. While John spoke out against theft, I think he smiled when he heard what the natives had done!

something to think about

1. Why did the natives want to get John off the island of Tanna? What did they think that John was changing and destroying?

2. Why did one of the chiefs say people should do as they pleased on the Lord's Day? Do people today still think they can do as they please on God's special day?

3. John's life was always in danger. What few words of Scripture gave him comfort in those times?
   Read Matthew 28:20

4. What was the name of John's faithful dog and how did he help to save John's life?

15
Kill Missi!

Some time after settling on Tanna John believed he had won the friendship of two chiefs – Nowar and Nerwangi. They, with some of their people, had begun to attend a simple worship service on the Lord's Day and even commenced Family Worship with their families. Nowar arranged a feast day with the villages within nine or ten miles of the harbour in honour of John and his God, Jehovah.

Almost one hundred men arrived for the feast. There was much talking by the fourteen chiefs and it was decided that war would be outlawed. They also agreed that their sacred men would not cast spells on people. John was very pleased with the decision but knew he could not depend on the decision they made.

Nowar and Nerwangi both indicated, 'This feast is held to move all the chiefs and people here to give up fighting, to become friends, and to worship your Jehovah God. We wish you to remain and to teach us all good conduct. As proof of our sincerity, and of our love, we have prepared this pile of food for you.'

After more dancing and shouting, which included a pretend fight between some warriors, men and women sat down to eat. John presented the chiefs with some fish hooks, knives and calico, but returned the cooked fowls and pigs because they had been first sacrificed to their chief pagan god.

John described the scene by writing, 'The dancing and fighting, the naked painted figures, and the constant yells and shouting, gave me a weird sensation and it seemed as if hell had broken loose.' The tribal members exchanged gifts and departed on friendly terms.

John now set to work improving the mission complex. He dug a well beside his house, striking water at four metres. When the natives saw the well filling with water, they were surprised to see 'rain rising up out of the earth'. With the help of some natives a building was constructed which was to be used for worship and as a school. He bought the timber from Aneityum, and paid for it with fifty pairs of trousers that had been sent to him from his Bible Class members in Glasgow. Often John had received gifts from his friends back home.

At first the people of Tanna were fearful of entering the church building, but soon five men, three women and three children were coming to worship, with John and his Christian teachers and their families.

On John's small printing press he was able to publish in the language of the people, the first page from the Scriptures. That night John danced for joy around his printing success. Next would be the teaching of the written language to the people of Tanna, so they could read the Scriptures for themselves.

John's next clash was with the sacred men of Tanna. The people believed that these men could control the weather, sickness and good health, and even life and death. Three sacred men stood up and said they did not believe in Jehovah and were more powerful that John or his God. They announced that they could kill John with their sorcery.

John took a piece of fruit from a woman standing nearby, and giving it to the three sacred men, told them to try and kill him using just a curse. They were not to attack him and kill him using spears or clubs. John said to them, 'You have seen me eat some of this fruit, and you have seen me give what was left to your sacred men. They have said they can kill me by Nahak (sorcery), but I challenge them to do it if they can, but not using an arrow, spear, club or gun. They have no power against me or anyone by their sorcery!'

Whenever John met the men he laughed at their powers, telling the men he was still very well.

The sacred men told the people of Tanna: 'We will delay killing Missi until all the sacred men are here. Then we will kill Missi before his next Lord's Day comes around. Let all watch, for he will soon die, and that without fail.'

'Very good!' said John. 'I challenge all your priests to unite and kill me by your sorcery. If I come to your village next Lord's Day in good health, you will admit that your gods have no power over me and that I am protected by the true and living Jehovah God!' Everyone kept watching John in case he fell ill, but finally everyone had to admit that John's God was more powerful than that of the sacred men.

John told the people that his God had protected him. He said that Jehovah was the living God, the one who answered the prayers of his people. He then took the opportunity to once again explain the way of salvation to the natives who were surprised that he was alive and well.

Suddenly one of the sacred men ran towards John, ready to throw his spear at him. Some natives grabbed the man while John said, 'Of course he can kill me with his spear, but he agreed to kill me by his magic, and promised he would not kill me using any war weapons. If you let him kill me you will have lost a good friend. If he kills me my God will be very angry.'

The man was unsure what he should do and followed John around for several weeks. However, God protected John and the sacred man gave up. Many natives now lost faith in their sacred men, who had been unable to kill John using their sorcery.

something to think about

1. Why were the natives afraid of the 'sacred men' of Tanna?

2. How did John humiliate the 'sacred men'?

3. John knew the importance of prayer. He also knew the importance of the one who answers prayer. Who did John say protected him? Another word for 'protect' is 'care'. **Read 1 Peter 5:7.** This verse explains very clearly about 'praying and being cared for'.

16
A visit to the Mathiesons

John would visit the Mathieson's whenever possible. Both husband and wife were in poor health, but they wanted to continue their work amongst the natives. On one occasion John received word that they had almost run out of flour and asked if he could bring them some.

John filled a large pot with flour. As war had broken out on the island and it was too dangerous to cross the island on foot, he decided to make the trip around the island by boat. The sea was too rough to use the mission boat so he asked Chief Nowar and Manuman, two friendly islanders, if they, and some of their men, would take him by canoe.

Old Chief Nowar

The pot of flour was made secure in the middle of the canoe and soon John with several natives, were making their way out to sea. The trip was very exciting as the waves were quite big and when it came to crossing the reef where some huge waves were breaking, the men said it was impossible to row properly but would make an attempt to beach the canoe.

Seeing a break in the big waves everyone paddled for the shore. However, a huge wave caught them and the canoe was thrown high into the air. Everyone, except John and the pot of flour, were thrown overboard. The natives, who were excellent swimmers, swam to the shore but when they saw that John was still in the canoe they swam out and dragged the canoe to the shore. When John opened the flour pot he found the contents safe and dry.

He then set off for the Mathieson's home, accompanied by a local native who carried the pot.

When they arrived at the mission house he spent several hours with his dear friends but all too soon it was time to leave for home. John was concerned that some warriors might be tempted to break into his home and steal his property.

He could not find any natives who would go with him on the journey across the island to his home. The sun was setting and he knew it would be very dangerous as the tribes were still fighting. The natives who lived close to the Mathieson's house said he was sure to be killed before he reached his home.

John set off, making sure he avoided any villages. When he heard voices approaching he stood still and didn't move until the natives had moved away.

At one spot he faced climbing a vertical pathway where one slip meant death on the rocks below. At another place he had to crawl along a cliff face to avoid being seen by some natives. When attempting to cross a valley he heard the voices of an unfriendly tribe.

Arriving at a place where he could not find any way to get down to the beach, he tried throwing rocks in an effort to find out how far below was the sand. However, John could not hear anything but the waves crashing on the rocks below. He knew he had to get down to the rocky shore, so commending himself to God sat down and launched himself down the cliff face. Without injury he landed with his feet in shallow water. He even found his umbrella which he had dropped from the top of the cliff face and thanked God for keeping him safe.

As he walked along the shore path the going became easier but he was still in great danger. When a group of armed natives appeared they thought he was one of the enemy and were about to fire at him with their muskets when John called out, 'I am Missi! Don't shoot; my love to you my friends!'

John offered them a gift of fish hooks if they would show him the shortest way back to his house, which they did. When he arrived home he had so much to thank God for. He had been kept safe through incredible dangers and his life had been spared to serve God and to take the message of salvation to those on the island.

The next day, when he told the friendly natives of his long walk during the night, they exclaimed, 'Surely, any of us would have been killed! Your Jehovah God alone protects you and has brought you safely home.'

John agreed with their words saying, 'Yes! and he will be your protector and helper too if only you will obey and trust him!'

Later John said that he could not have faced the canoe journey or the walk home, had he not felt secure that he was doing what the Lord wanted him to do. He knew the Lord cared for his people and he could say with the apostle Paul, 'I can do all things through Christ who strengthens me.'

something to think about

1. This chapter of the book is full of the incredible dangers that John went through. But at each stage, God was looking after him.
   We never know how many times we may have come to harm but for the Lord's protection. What did the crowds do to Paul that may have killed him?
   Read Acts 14:19-20.

2. **In Philippians 4:13 Paul says, 'I can do all things through Christ who stregthens me.'**
   How do you think the Christian gets strength from God, especially during the difficult times? We have spoken about this before and it was something that John did many times during his life.

17
A bad case of measles

After almost two years on Tanna a ship arrived bringing two new missionaries to help with the work on the island. They were a Canadian couple – Samuel and Elizabeth Johnston. John enjoyed the company of this couple and together they prayed for God to open the hearts of the people to receive the gospel. Samuel and Elizabeth spent much of their time learning the local language. John taught them about fifteen new words each day and soon they were helping John as he went about the villages teaching the people of Jehovah and the Lord Jesus Christ.

The arrival in the harbour of four trading ships was to cause much trouble for the natives on the island. The captain of one said, 'We know how to humble your proud Tannese now! We'll humble them in front of you!'

'Surely you don't meant to attack and destroy these poor people,' replied John, who thought the sailors would invade the villages, killing the people wherever they went.

This was not to be as the ships' captains had a far more horrible way of killing people than John had ever imagined.

They put on shore at different places, four men who were suffering from the measles. Unlike Europeans the natives had no resistance to the disease, and an attack of measles usually meant death. The traders also invited on board Kapuku, a young native friend of Mr and Mrs Mathieson. The sailors grabbed him and locked him below deck with some natives who had bad cases of the disease. When the sun was about to set he was released and at once he made his way back to his village, carrying the sickness with him.

Soon the disease had spread throughout the villages and almost one third of the Tannese died. John and the Johnstons visited the sick, giving them water to drink and providing medicines and food.

Often the natives, burning with fever, ran down into the ocean for coolness. But the shock of the cold water caused them to collapse and drown. Some dug a trench on the beach and covered themselves with the cool, wet sand, but again they died from shock. They had dug their own graves!

Thirteen of John's helpers from Aneityum died and the rest packed their belongings and returned home. As they were boarding the 'John Knox' John asked old Abraham, 'Are you also going to leave me here alone on Tanna to fight the battles of the Lord?'

Abraham had thought that John was about to join him on the ship so he said, 'Missi, will you remain?'

When John replied that he could not leave his work on Tanna, Abraham turned about and took his belongings back to the house. Abraham said to John, 'Then Missi, I remain with you of my own free will, and with all my heart. We will live and die together in the work of the Lord. I will never leave you while you are spared on Tanna!'

John knew his companions were in danger from the locals who blamed all white people for what had happened.

One night when Abraham, John and Samuel and Elizabeth Johnston were about to go to their rooms for a night's rest when they saw two warriors outside, painted with war paint and carrying huge clubs. They asked for 'medicine for a sick boy'.

He invited them into the room, but they refused and John knew they had come to kill the missionaries. John prepared the medicine that was needed and when he offered it to the men, they entered the room and started to swing their clubs about.

John told them, 'You see that Mr Johnston is now leaving and you too must leave this room for tonight. Tomorrow, you can bring the boy or come for the medicine.'

John showed them the door, following Mr Johnston who had gone before them. As he bent down to pick up a small kitten, one man swung his club at him. Mr Johnston was not hit, but fell to the ground as he ducked the blows. When John set his two dogs on them the men ran away but John called after them, 'Remember, Jehovah God sees you and will punish you for trying to murder his servants!'

As the men ran a number of warriors who had been hiding outside followed them. They had all come to kill the missionaries and probably burn their building.

This kind of thing had happened to John before but Samuel Johnston was so bothered that he could not sleep well. He continued to accompany John when he visited the villages but when he fell ill it was found that he had tetanus from an infected wound. Soon he was unable to walk and it was necessary to force his mouth open in order to give him food and water.

Three weeks later Samuel died and John and Elizabeth laid his body to rest in a grave near that of Mary and Peter. Elizabeth returned to Aneityum, where she taught in a school for almost three years. She married John's good friend, Joseph Copeland and they later moved to the island of Fortuna where they spent the rest of their lives teaching the natives of salvation in the Lord Jesus.

something to think about

1. The captain of a trading ship thought of a horrible way to kill
    the natives. What was it?

2. It was very sad when a large number of the natives on
    Tanna died from catching the measles. But remember what
    the final punishment is for all who do not believe in the
    Lord Jesus Christ?
    Read Luke 13:3-5. The end of verse 5 should help you
    with your answer.

3. But there is a way out for those who trust the Lord Jesus
    Christ as their Saviour.
    Read Luke 15:3-7. Jesus here tells us a parable about a
    Lost Sheep. This parable shows how God feels about repent-
    ant sinners – those who are truly sorry for their sins?
    At the end of verse 6, what does God say he will do when
    even one sinner repents?

18
More deaths

Some years before the outbreak of the measles plague, a young Tannese chief named Kowia had gone to Aneityum where he was converted. He had been taught much about Christianity and had a desire to return to Tanna with his new wife and two children. He wanted to tell his own people of the Lord Jesus Christ who had lived and died to save sinners.

He brought his family back to Tanna and proved a great help to John and Abraham. The islanders who knew him, ordered him to throw aside his Christian faith and abandon John and Abraham. However, Kowia replied, 'I shall stand by Missi and the worship of Jehovah!'

When some natives sold him some fowls for the mission, they were stolen and then offered to John. Kowia called out to John, 'Don't buy them Missi! I have just bought them for you, and paid for them!'

The natives looked on and some began calling out that Kowia was a coward. Kowia was upset by this and spoke to John: 'Missi, they think that because I am now a Christian I have become a coward, a woman, to bear every abuse and insult they can heap on me! But I will show them now that I am no coward and am still their chief. They will learn that Christianity does not take away but gives us courage!'

Grabbing a big club from a nearby warrior he turned to the crowd and called out, 'Come, any of you, come all against your chief! My Jehovah God makes my heart and arms strong.

He will help me in this battle as he helps me in other things, for he inspires me to show you that Christians are no cowards, though they are men of peace. Come on and you will yet know that I am Kowia, your chief!'

Moving towards the men who had insulted him, Kowia found them backing away. 'Who are the cowards now?' he shouted. Kowia had no more trouble from his people.

Not long after Samuel Johnston's death, John fell ill and was cared for by Abraham and Kowia. One day John awoke to find Kowia beside him. He said, 'Missi, all our Aneityumese are sick. Missi Johnston is dead. You are very sick and I am weak and dying. Alas, when I too am dead, who will climb the tree and get you a coconut to drink? And who will bathe your lips and brow?'

Kowia burst into tears but continued, 'Missi, the Tanna-men hate us all on account of the worship of Jehovah; and now I fear he is going to take away all his servants from this land and leave my people to the evil one.'

John was too sick to reply but listened as Kowia prayed, 'O Lord, our Father in heaven, are you going to take away all your servants and your worship from this dark land? What do you mean to do O Lord? The Tannese hate you and your worship and your servants; but surely O Lord, you cannot forsake Tanna and leave our people to die in darkness! Oh, make the hearts of this people soft to your word and sweet to your worship; teach them to fear and love Jesus; and Oh, restore and spare Missi, dear Missi Paton, that Tanna may be saved!'

Those words thrilled John because they came from a man who had once practised cannibalism.

Several days later Kowia came to John again, saying, 'Missi, I am very weak; I am dying. I come to bid you farewell, and go away to die ..'

During John's illness Kowia's wife and children had died and now he asked to be buried beside them. His last words to

John were, 'I am happy, looking to Jesus. Farewell Missi ... we will meet again in Jesus and with Jesus.'

During the outbreak of the measles, the white traders blamed it on John and his missionary companions. They said there would be no more trading until the Christians were driven from Tanna.

In early 1861, while the natives were recovering from the measles plague, the island was swept with a series of wild storms which destroyed much of the food crops. Houses were blown down and some villages destroyed by the strong winds. Many canoes were wrecked on the coral reef around the harbour.

On the other side of the island the bigger portion of the Mathieson's house was destroyed. Despite the wild storm and rain, John had to stand guard over his house to prevent the natives from stealing his possessions.

When the war-chief Miaki's baby son died, four men were murdered so their spirits could accompany the child into the next world and take care of him. John was threatened with death and his house was surrounded by armed natives who broke down the fences and cut down the few banana trees left standing after the storm. They also stole his fowls and several goats that provided him with milk.

In the months that followed wars broke out and about thirteen warriors who had been killed in the fighting were cooked and eaten. Several tribes refused to become involved in the cannibalism, having believed John's teaching. However, they had no problem in giving the bodies to other tribes for them to cook and eat. They exchanged the bodies for pigs that roamed the inland part of the island.

John's life was in danger and even Chief Nowar became fearful of what was likely to happen and gave up attending the Lord's Day worship service. The natives believed that their pagan gods were angry for allowing the missionaries to live. Now life for John and his companions was very dangerous.

something to think about

1. What do we learn from the behaviour of Chief Kowia who
    returned to Tanna?
    Read 2 Corinthians 5:17. This will tell you what Chief
    Kowia became after his conversion.

2. What were the chief's final words to John?
    Where will all believers meet again and who also will be
    there?
    Read about this in Philippians 3:20-21

3. Why was John so thrilled to hear the prayer of Kowia?

19
Tanna visited by a 'man-of-war'

On the nearby island of Erromanga the measles plague had also killed many natives. The traders blamed the missionaries and their God Jehovah for all the deaths, with the result that Rev George Gordon and his wife were killed.

The traders then gave the warriors from Erromanga a boat which they used to visit Tanna. Here they urged the natives to kill John and his Christian helpers. This they said would rid the islands of Christianity.

At a feast held with the natives from Erromanga Chief Nowar, John's friend, again put on his war-paint and went back to his pagan ways. Armed with his weapons he warned John, 'If they are not punished for what has been done on Erromanga, nothing else can keep them here from killing you and me, and all who worship at the mission house.' He began to have doubts about his faith and said, 'How is it that Jehovah did not protect the Gordons and the Erromangan worshippers? If the Erromangans are not punished, neither will our Tannese be punished, even if they murder all of Jehovah's people!'

Abraham remained loyal to John and Jehovah, and prayed for protection... 'Our great King, protect us, and make their hearts soft and sweet to your worship. Or, if they are permitted to kill us … wash us in the blood of your dear Son Jesus Christ. He came down to earth and shed his blood for sinners; through him forgive us our sins and take us to heaven… Our Lord, our hearts are pained just now, and we weep over the death of your dear servants; but make our hearts good and strong for your cause, and take away all our fears. Make us two, and all your servants, strong for you and for your worship; and if they kill us two, let us die together in your good work, like your servants Missi Gordon the man and Missi Gordon the woman.'

Miaki, the war chief, called for the death of John and came to the mission house with some armed warriors. He encouraged other tribes to kill Mr and Mrs Mathieson on the other side of the island.

When the trading ship 'Blue Bell' entered the harbour, some warriors approached John and warned him, 'This is one of the vessels that brought the measles. You and they made the sickness and destroyed our people. Now if you do not leave with this ship, we will kill you all!'

John knew they were trying to frighten him away from the house so they could steal everything. He reminded them how his medicine had helped many of them recover from the measles. He had then shown the natives how to make a fishing net and they caught more fish than ever before. The extra fish were used to barter pigs from the inland tribes, making up for the crops that were destroyed in the storms.

Miaki was furious that John was winning the affection of many natives. On one occasion John arrived home just in time to prevent his house being set alight. A cousin of Miaki gave John some poisonous fish which he claimed were good for eating. Chief Nowar saw what was taking place and warned him just in time to prevent him eating the deadly fish.

John continued teaching the people Biblical truths. As he had printed some pages of the Scriptures he began to teach the people to read. He commenced with the alphabet, offering a prize of a red shirt to the first person who could repeat it by heart. It was an Inikahi chief who won the prize and then commenced teaching others.

'A is a man's legs with the body cut off; ...C is a three-quarters moon;... E is a man with one club under his feet and another over his head...' and so on. 'I have taught my little child, who can scarcely walk, the names of them all,' the chief told his listeners. 'You will soon learn to read the book, if you try it with all your heart!'

Again Miaki caused John trouble, claiming that he could destroy a man-of-war even if one came to the island. 'Miaki will make a great wind and sink any man-of-war that comes here. We will take the man-of-war and kill all that are on board. If you and Abraham do not leave us we will kill you both, for we must have the traders.'

Just then the mission ship 'John Knox' was sighted coming into the harbour, followed by two large battleships, or men-of war.

John turned to the crowd and challenged them: 'Now is your time! Make all possible haste! Let Miaki raise his great wind now; get all your men ready; I will tell them that you mean to fight, and you will find them always ready!'

With that the natives turned and ran for the trees. Chief Nowar refused to come and meet the ships' captains. When they came ashore the captains offered to take John to Aneityum, or wherever he wanted to go. However, he said that he would remain at Tanna and carry on with his God-given work.

The captains met with the local island chiefs and warned them of the consequences of harming a missionary. One of the local chiefs, Nouka, explained the problem: 'We love Missi. But when the traders tell us that the worship makes us sick, and when they bribe us with tobacco and powder to kill him or drive him away, some believe them and our hearts do bad conduct to Missi.'

The chiefs were invited on board a man-of-war where they saw the firing of the big guns. They were impressed and promised not to harm John, but soon after the ships left the harbour, threats were again made against the Christians. Even Chief Nowar said that as he was not present when the promises were made, he could do as he pleased to John and his helpers.

something to think about

1. Chief Nowar accuses God of not taking care of the Gordons and the Erromangan Christians. But sometimes God does allow believers to be hurt or even killed.
   Read about the death of Stephen in Acts 7:54-60.
   We may not understand the reasons but we must remember that God always does what is right.

2. Miaki boasts that he has power over the wind. We know that there is only one who has that power.
   Read about it in Matthew 8:23-27

3. Why did John want to teach the natives to read? Do you think that the symbols in the alphabet were a clever way of writing down the language?

20
John – the centre of attention

War was in the air and armed groups strode about in each village square, ready for the word to be given to attack. Much of their hatred was directed at John. However, Ian, an inland chief, wanted John to stay on Tanna. Miaki and Nouka, coastal chiefs, said to Ian, 'If you will keep Missi and his worship, take him with you to your land, for we will not have him live at the harbour.'

To this, Ian leapt to his feet and shouted, 'On whose land does Missi live, yours or ours? Who fights against the worship and all good, who are the thieves and murderers, who tell lies – you or we?'

Ian then angrily said that the land on which the mission was built belonged to his tribe: 'The land was not yours to sell,' he told them. 'It was really ours. Your fathers stole it from us long ago by war; but we would not have asked it back had you not asked us to take Missi away. Now we will defend him on it and he will teach us and our people in our own land!'

Ian begged John to come to the meeting of chiefs and warriors. John was fearful of what might happen to him but when he arrived he found a well armed squad of Ian's men. They faced a rather fearful Miaki, Nouka and their less well-armed warriors. Ian led John to the space between the two groups and pointing to his own warriors, said: 'Missi, these are my men and your friends! We are here to defend you and the worship… These', he said, pointing to the other group of men, 'are your enemies and ours! … Missi, say the word, and the muskets of my men will sweep all opposition away and the worship will spread and we will all be stronger for it on Tanna.'

But John could only give one answer: '... I am here to teach you how to turn away from all wickedness, to worship and serve Jehovah and to live in peace. How can I approve of any person being killed for me or for the worship? My God would be angry with me and punish me if I did!'

John then warned them all of hurting a servant of Jehovah, and urged everyone to turn to the Lord Jesus for salvation. Ian, however, was not satisfied: 'Missi, they will kill you! They will kill us and you will be to blame.' Miaki and Nouka saw this as an opportunity to avoid a war and shouted, 'Missi's word is good! Let us all obey it. Let us all worship!' Little more was said, and with the exchange of peace offerings, the flames of war were extinguished for the time being.

When Chief Ian fell ill, John suspected that he was being poisoned but Miaki and Nouka boasted publicly that he was being killed by their evil spell. John was called to Chief Ian's bedside where he discovered that he had a large knife with which he intended to kill him. Suddenly he threw the knife aside and told John, 'Go, go quickly.' John left the hut and ran for his life. Ian could not bring himself to kill John.

When Ian did eventually die, the men killed two of his wives and placing the three bodies on a canoe, buried them in the ocean. But the plot devised by Miaki and Nouka had not turned out as planned. The natives had wanted Ian to kill John, then Ian would die from poison. If a British man-of-war arrived and the captain wanted to know what had happened to John, Ian would be dead and there would be no one to punish. Killing and revenge played such a large part of island life.

Chief Miaki was still boasting that his sacred man had successfully killed Ian and now boasted that he could destroy any property that belonged to his enemies. He even claimed the power to call up great storms to destroy the villages and crops on the island.

Not long after this boast a storm did in fact strike the island and caused much damage to the side of the island where Ian's tribe lived. Ian's warriors decided to avenge their dead chief, whom they believed had been killed by Miaki's sacred man. War broke out between the two tribes.

John and Abraham were told to remain in the mission complex and they would not be harmed. However, when bullets began whizzing past their home they discovered that Miaki's men were using it as a shelter from their enemy. Loud screaming came from the bush all around and when old Chief Nowar came to help John, he was wounded with a spear to his knee. His men carried him back to his village amid great shouts of victory from the enemy.

With Nowar out of the way, some natives smashed their way into the mission buildings, broke open boxes and stole everything they could, including John's boat. During this assault, John and his companions were in a bedroom praying that the Lord would save them from the pagan natives who wanted all the missionaries dead.

One chief, pretending to be willing to care for John, called out but when John came to the window, the man shouted, 'Come on, let's kill him now!' A tomahawk suddenly came through the window just missing him. When John tried to stop the attack by warning the warriors that Jehovah would punish them for what they were doing, someone cried out, 'It's all lies about the man-of-war. They didn't punish the Erromangans. They are afraid of us! Come on, let us kill them!'

John and his companions were surrounded by warriors but when he produced a revolver, which Joseph Copeland had left with him to use as a threat, the natives stood still as one shouted out, 'Missi has a short musket! He will shoot us all!' Hearing those words the natives fell to the ground. When they thought they were safe they turned and ran for the bush where the shouting and screaming continued.

something to think about

1. Miaki is boasting again. In this chapter he says that he can make storms destroy villages and crops. Miaki also says that he and Nouka can kill people by their evil spells. Miaki continues to boast throughout the book – he is a very boastful man. But their boasts and plans went very wrong when Ian failed to kill John.
   We read in the Bible about people whose plans went wrong. Joseph's brothers planned to kill him but Judah could not do this. Instead Joseph's life was spared and he was sold to the Ishmalites. Later on Joseph became second-in-command to Pharaoh.
   Read about this in Genesis 37:12-36

2. Who controls the affairs of this world? **Read Psalm 115:3 and Psalm 135:6.** What is the same phrase used in both of these readings.

21
The Lord to the rescue

Later that night John and his companions made their way to the village of two local chiefs – Miaki and Nouka. These men had stolen all of John and Abraham's belongings but their accusations were treated with silence.

Eventually Miaki spoke, 'Missi, where was Jehovah today? There was no Jehovah today to protect you. It's all lies about Jehovah. We will come and kill you, and Abraham, and his wife, and cut your bodies into pieces to be cooked and eaten in every village upon Tanna.'

But John replied, 'Surely, when you had planned all this, and brought them to kill us and steal our property, Jehovah did protect us, or we would not have been here!'

Miaki, however, continued to boast: 'There is no Jehovah today! We have no fear of any man-of-war. They dare not punish us… They will talk to us and say we must not do so again, and give us a present. That's all. We fear nothing. The talk of all Tanna is that we will kill you and seize all your property tomorrow.'

Leaving the warriors, John sent word to Chief Nowar asking what he should do. The reply came, inviting him to Nowar's village where an effort would be made to protect the missionaries. John, Abraham, his wife and Matthew knew they would be murdered if they stayed at the mission building. Grabbing what was left of their property, and accompanied by Clutha, they quickly made their way to Nowar's village. John was sorry to see Mary's piano, silverware, a box of medicines, and the clothes that had been sent to him by the members of his Glasgow Bible Study group, all left behind for the natives to steal.

When they reached Nowar's village they realised they were being followed by Miaki's warriors who had discovered the mission house empty. Women with their children ran to hide in the bush and old Chief Nowar called John to him saying, 'Missi, sit down beside me, and pray to our Jehovah God, for if he does not send deliverance now we are all dead men. They will kill us all on your account, and that quickly. Pray, and I will watch!'

As John prayed Nowar watched the approaching warriors. Suddenly they stood still about three hundred yards from the village. Nowar touched John's knee saying, 'Missi, Jehovah is hearing, they are all standing still.'

Suddenly a warrior arrived and spoke to his companions who all turned about and returned the way they had come. Later Nowar told his people, 'Jehovah heard Missi's prayer! Jehovah has protected us and turned them away back.'

John said afterwards, 'I don't know why they turned back; but I have no doubt it was the doing of God to save our lives.' He joined the others in giving praise and thanks to God for saving them yet again from what seemed to be certain death.

After a couple of days John and his companions decided to make their way to the Mathieson's home on the other side of the island. Nowar told John to climb a tree and hide there in case more warriors came to attack. Up the tree, John felt secure. Even though he was alone he knew that he was not alone for the Lord Jesus was watching over him. A true sense of security and peace flooded his heart and mind.

About midnight, word came for the missionaries to make their way to the shore where they would escape to the Mathieson's by boat. Even though the payment for the canoe had been made, the builder demanded more! He wanted extra payment for an axe, a sail and a pair of blankets. John used the last of his goods to pay for the extra equipment, only to be asked for further payment for the paddles.

John threatened to walk across the island to the Mathieson's home but Nowar's men produced paddles from the village, and at last the four missionaries, accompanied by a native boy to navigate, launched the boat and set off. When they reached the open sea the wind was blowing strongly and they faced rough seas.

Abraham believed they were doomed, and putting down his paddle, called out, 'Missi, we are all drowned now! We are food for the sharks.'

John quickly took a paddle, ordered Abraham to take one and asked the others to start bailing. To Abraham he called out, 'Abraham, where is your faith in Jesus now? Remember, he is ruler on sea and land. Abraham, pray and paddle hard! Keep up stroke for stroke with me, as our lives depend on it. Our God can protect us! Matthew, bail with all your might. Don't look around on the sea and be afraid. Let us pray to God and paddle, and he will save us yet!' Abraham said he had been wrong: 'Thank you for that, Missi. I will be strong. I pray to God and will paddle. God will save us!'

After five hours in the open ocean, they turned the boat to the shore and landed at the same spot from which they had left. The missionaries were so tired and sore that they lay down and fell asleep.

John awoke when he felt someone trying to steal the bag he was using as a pillow. It contained his Bible and the pages of Scripture he had printed in Tannese. When John jumped to his feet the man ran away.

John, Abraham and his wife, and Matthew knelt down on the sand, thanking God for rescuing them from the ocean and seeking guidance as to what they should do next. The situation was very dangerous and they knew that they might be murdered at any moment.

something to think about

1. What does old Chief Nowar tell John to do while he watches out for the warriors? Jesus tells his disciples to do both of these things.
    Read Matthew 26:40-46. Did the disciples do as they were asked?

2. Was Abraham afraid when they were in the boat?
    Read John 6:16-21. Were the disciples afraid of the storm and what did Jesus do this time to show them he was in total control of the situation?

3. What did John and his friends do when God rescued them from the ocean? Do we always remember to do this?

22
A dangerous journey!

While they thought about their next move, Nowar's son-in-law, Faimungo appeared, warning them that Miaki and his men were coming to kill them all. Because of the danger, the missionaries said they would follow Faimungo, as they knew his village was in the direction they wanted to go.

At first they only met friendly natives but suddenly after walking about four miles they found themselves surrounded by Miaki's men. Faimungo waved his spear, saying, 'No! You shall not kill Missi today. He is with me!' Then he walked on with John's party following.

The native, Sirawia, who was in charge of the armed men, shouted out at Faimungo, 'Your conduct is bad in taking Missi away. Leave him to us to be killed!'

John then reminded him of the kindness the Christians had shown to them all: 'Sirawia, I love you all. You must know that I sought only your good. I gave you medicine and food when you and your people were sick and dying from the measles; I gave you the very clothing you wear. Am I not your friend? Have we not often drunk tea and eaten together in my house? Can you stand there and see your friend shot? If you do, my God will punish you severely.'

John and his companions gradually walked carefully through the natives. When they were out of their reach they turned and ran for their lives.

Reaching a settlement near Faimungo's village they heard another party of armed warriors approaching. Soon the Christians found themselves encircled by angry natives. One threw a stone used to kill people, but when it grazed Abraham's cheek he gazed up into the heavens as if to say, 'Missi, I was nearly called away to Jesus!'

The warriors began encouraging each other to kill John but suddenly the peace of God filled his heart and mind.

Later John said, 'I realised that I could not die until my Master's work with me was done. The assurance came to me, as if a voice out of heaven had spoken, that not a musket would be fired to wound us, not a club strike us, not a spear leave the hand in which it was held, not an arrow leave the bow, or a killing stone the fingers, without the permission of Jesus Christ, who has all power in heaven and on earth. He rules all nature … and restrains even the savages of the South Seas.'

Facing death he was reminded of Christ's promise, ' Lo, I am with you always...' John and his friends could confidently say, 'For I am persuaded that neither death nor life ... nor any other created thing, shall be able to separate us from the love of God which is in Christ Jesus our Lord.'

After some talking, Faimungo and his warriors led the way, John and his companions following. Behind them all followed a group of armed men. When John became separated from Faimungo in a creek, he heard stones crashing into the trees beside him. He knew that his enemy was close at hand.

Crawling out of the creek, John ran after his protectors and coming to a native village he walked close to Faimungo, as no one dared risk throwing a weapon and hitting the chief.

When some villagers said Miaki told them that the Christians had caused the storms and measles disease, Faimungo said, 'They lie about Missi! It is our own bad conduct that makes us sick.'

When the armed natives threatened to kill John, Faimungo stood between him and the men saying, 'You won't kill Missi today!'

Approaching the boundary of his land, Faimungo said to John, 'Missi, I have now fulfilled my promise. I am so tired, I am so afraid, I dare not go any further.'

Before he turned to go his own way, he pointed to a track, saying, 'You must keep straight along that path.'

When two armed natives appeared, John took out his revolver and said to them, 'Beware! Lay down your spears at once on the sand and carry my bag to the next land boundary!' At once the young men did as they were told. Reaching the boundary markers they put down John's basket and asked, 'Missi, let us return to our home!'

Arriving at the Mathieson's home they found the two missionaries sick and very sad because their only child had just died. However they were overjoyed to meet John and his companions.

John told them he had left a letter with Chief Nowar which was to be handed to the captain of any ship which called at the harbour. They prayed that the Lord would send a ship, but when one did appear, it sailed on. John waved a flag but the captain took no notice of the attempts to attract his attention.

The Mathiesons continued to conduct worship each Lord's Day, and with the new arrivals, they visited the local villagers, teaching them of the Lord Jesus Christ. At one spot where the road came to a fork, a native leapt out with his club raised, ready to hit John over the head. Mr Mathieson yelled out a warning, which caused him to turn around and grab the club from his attacker. He then ordered the native to lead the way home. Arriving home, John returned the native's club, and he disappeared into the trees.

something to think about

1. John reminded the warrior Sirawia that the Christians had done many things to help the natives. Can you name what they were?

2. John and his friends knew that they would not be killed until they had done the work God planned for them. He knew that they were God's fellow workers.
   Paul compared the work he was doing to that of a farmer. **Read 1 Corinthians 3:5-9.** John and his friends were planting and watering – but who made things grow?

3. John knew that he could not be separated from the love of God. What passage of Scripture encouraged John when he was confronted with possible death? You will find it in this chapter.
   Read it in full in Romans 8:35-39

23
God's sends rain and the 'Blue Bell' to the rescue!

Some natives reported that trading ships had called at the harbour where John lived, and there exchanged all the missionary's possessions for guns and weapons. They also heard that Miaki had been moving about, inciting the people to kill all the Christians.

One night John was awakened by Clutha his faithful dog, who was barking loudly. Quietly looking out the window, John could see that the house was completely surrounded by the natives who had set fire to the fence and some church buildings. John realised if something was not done quickly their house would be going up in flames.

With his revolver in one hand and tomahawk in the other, he had Mr Mathieson quietly open the door and let him out. Everyone watched and prayed as John ran towards the burning fence. Quickly he knocked it to the ground where it could do no damage to the house. John saw eight or more warriors in the shadows, and heard one call out, 'Kill him! Kill him!'

When the armed men encircled John, with clubs held up, ready to fall on his head, he took out his revolver and said, 'Dare you strike me? If you do, my Jehovah God will punish you. He protects us and will punish you for burning his church, for hatred to his worship and people, and for all your bad conduct. We love you all; and for doing you good you want to kill us! But our God is here now to protect us and to punish you.'

Suddenly everyone was aware of a roaring sound coming their way. When the tornado struck, the flames were blown away from the buildings. Then the heavens opened and rain began to fall.

The natives were quiet. When one called out, 'That is Jehovah's rain! Truly their Jehovah God is fighting for them and helping them. Let us all get away from this place!' With that the warriors all turned and ran for their lives. When they had all gone John returned to the house and called out, 'Open and let me in. I am now all alone!'

As Mr Mathieson let John in he said, 'If ever, in time of need, God sent help and protection to his servants in answer to prayer, he did so tonight!' Then everyone bowed down and gave thanks to a faithful God for sending the wind and rain to save them from the anger of the natives.

It was difficult to sleep that night. John lay awake most of the time listening. Clutha kept watch at his side with his ears pricked to catch any sound. However, all was quiet. The next morning some natives arrived with the news that many armed warriors were on their way to kill the missionaries, loot the buildings and burn them to the ground.

John and his friends committed themselves to God and waited the arrival of the warriors. Just as they heard them approaching, the cry went up, 'Sail O! Sail O!' At the moment of their greatest danger God had once again come to their rescue by sending the 'Blue Bell' to their side of the island. To make sure they were seen, John set fire to some reeds which made a lot of smoke, and tied a white sheet to one end of the building and a black shawl to the other.

The captain had been asked by John's friends at Aneityum to call and see if all was well on Tanna. Soon a party of twenty well armed men had come ashore and made their way to the house. Before long one boat was transporting some of the Mathieson's possessions to the 'Blue Bell'. The other men helped the missionaries pack. When they were ready to leave, Mr Mathieson locked himself in his study and refused to come out. He had decided to remain and become a martyr.

It took a lot of persuasion on the part of John to get Mr Mathieson to leave, but when he finally did, they could not see the 'Blue Bell' and found that it had left before the tide changed. John and Mr Mathieson made their way to Port Resolution, which was close to John's mission station.

Here one boat decided to stay while the other again set out to sea to find the 'Blue Bell'. During the afternoon a canoe, carrying Chief Miaki and Chief Nowar, pulled alongside and tried to persuade John and the others to come ashore, promising that there would be no danger. This proved to be false, because when Abraham and some armed men went ashore, they saw armed warriors waiting to attack John if he came to the beach. They also saw that John's buildings had be smashed and his possessions stolen. In fact John had seen some of the sailors from the 'Blue Bell' wearing his clothes which had been sold to them by the natives.

When Miaki realised that John was not coming ashore he said, 'We have taken everything your house contained, and would take you too if we could, for we hate the worship. It causes all our diseases and deaths; it goes against our customs, and condemns the things we enjoy.'

That evening the 'Blue Bell' appeared and when everything was stored aboard, the ship set sail for Aneityum. The captain refused to accept any fare from the missionaries, so the money was given to the sailors as a gift for their help and kindness.

something to think about

1. In this chapter God sends both rain and the 'Blue Bell' to rescue John. In the Bible God sometimes saves his people from harm or death by sending totally unexpected happenings. Remember how God saved Daniel from being eaten by the lions.
    Read about this in Daniel 6:10-23.

2. Can you remember a time, when as a boy, God kept David safe? Who was David fighting?
    Read about this in 1 Samuel 17:1-10 and 33-51.

3. The next time it rains or there is a flood, remember that these are under the control of God. But God has promised that never again will he destroy all life as he did in the flood.
    Read Genesis 9:12-17. What does God promise in verse 15?

24
Australia

John wanted to remain on Aneityum and continue with his translation of the Bible into Tannese. He hoped that one day, when it was safe, he would be able to return to Tanna. The other missionaries however, including his friend Joseph Copeland, persuaded him to visit Australia where he could tell the churches about the desperate need of mission support for the work in the New Hebrides. They urgently needed more workers and also money to purchase a new boat.

For £10 John was able to obtain passage to Australia on a sandalwood trading ship. The 1,400 mile voyage was hard going. The captain was a cruel man, who, with his native wife, occupied the only cabin. There was much swearing and fighting amongst the crew, and the natives, who were forced to work, were to be sold in Australia as slaves to work on the sugar plantations of Queensland. John spent most days and nights on deck. He had nowhere to wash and his food was not fit for a dog to eat.

John disembarked in Sydney. Before long he met a kind Christian couple, Mr and Mrs Foss, who invited him to be a guest in their home. They introduced him to Christians and ministers who invited him to speak about the needs of the missionary work in the New Hebrides.

Soon he was speaking in churches to congregations and Sunday schools. He formed a committee of well known and respected people to handle all donations to the mission-field and commenced a wonderful scheme for raising money for a new ship. Every child who gave 6d (six old pence) to the work of the mission, received a share certificate. This meant that they each owned a very small part of the ship. Children and their parents were caught up in the scheme, using money boxes to store their savings. John called it 'The Shipping Company for Jesus.'

As John travelled about in south eastern Australia he also asked for money to support native pastors like Abraham. When money poured in for this work some churches and Sunday schools were able to adopt a native minister as their own.

John always took with him a bag containing articles owned and worn by the natives on Tanna. He used these to illustrate his talks and to help people understand what life was really like in the New Hebrides.

John then set about visiting the Australian outback. Frequently he became lost and on one occasion he walked into a bog and became trapped. Had his cries for help not been heard, he would have been dead by morning time.

On another occasion he began speaking to a passenger on the stagecoach on which they were travelling.

The man, a Scot asked, 'Are you a minister?'

'Yes,' John replied.

'Where is your church?' the man wanted to know.

'I have no church,' came the reply.

'Where then is your home?' he was asked.

'I have no home,' John replied.

'Where have you come from?' was the next question.

'The South Sea Islands,' John replied.

'What then are you doing in Australia?' the man asked.

'Pleading for help for the mission,' John again replied.

'Are you a Presbyterian?' the man asked.

'I am,' John said,

With that the Scot insisted paying John's coach fare.

On one outback cattle station John was met by an Irish Catholic who ordered him off his property. John quietly answered, 'I'm sorry if my arrival has upset you, but I wish you every blessing in Christ Jesus. Good-bye!' Before John could leave the man's wife called out, 'Don't let that missionary go away!' She had heard John speak in Melbourne and wanted to know what he carried in his bag.

John returned and for some time showed both husband and wife the articles he had brought with him from Tanna and else- where. Before he left, the land owner gave him £5 and wished him well.

On another occasion he was running late for a talk and was given a racehorse by the name of 'Garibaldi' to ride. The owner said, 'Point him in the right direction and let him go! We'll get him back sometime later. He knows the way!'

John wasn't a good horse rider and when three men on horseback overtook him, they laughed at him. However, Garibaldi was not going to stand for that and began racing towards the three men on horseback. Soon he had passed them and continued to gallop on to the property he knew. All John could do was grimly hang on.

Garibaldi came to a stop at the homestead door. John dismounted and, covered in mud, walked a few steps like a drunken person into the home. He was so shocked he could not speak properly.

The farmer suggested he change his clothes but John said they were to arrive later on the stagecoach. With that the farmer gave him a change of his own clothing, which, when he put them on, made him look ridiculous. When they all sat down to the evening meal, John tried to explain what had happened. The people knew 'Garibaldi' very well and found the story very amusing.

something to think about

1. John met some very kind people in Sydney who invited him to stay in their home. What were their names? Are we always kind to strangers that we may meet?
    In Genesis 18:1-15 we read about Abraham and the three men he entertained in his tent. Two of these are angels. Do you know who the third man was?

2. What scheme did John set up while in Australia? The children gave some of their pocket money each week to help buy the ship. Think how you could give some money each week to help those in other countries.

3. We see in this chapter that John told the Scotsman he had no home. We read about another man named John in the Bible who also owned very little.
    Read Mark 1:1-8 to find out more about him. What was his family relationship to Jesus?

25
John meets some Australian Aborigines

It was during one of his outback journeys that John first met some Australian Aborigines. He saw a large crowd one Lord's Day, gathered for a day's sport. However, before long, fighting had broken out and the noise disrupted the church service. In the afternoon he made his way to their camp where he spoke to some. Over a cup of tea and some damper (rough bread; just flour, water and salt, usually cooked in the coals of the camp fire), John spoke to them of the Saviour, the Lord Jesus Christ.

They were not used to being shown much kindness by white people. In some parts of Australia white people even shot Aborigines for their drunken behaviour, although they had sold the Aborigines alcohol in exchange for blankets. They also punished the Aborigines for the theft of sheep or cattle. This made John very angry and he wrote about this: 'And their sin, their crime? Oh, because of hunger, only seizing a sheep, which fattened on the lands that once grew their food, and from which the white man had pitilessly hunted them.'

Even those children who were taken from their tribe and taught to work as household servants, were often very badly treated. Some white people believed the Aborigines to be little better than animals, not worth teaching, and unworthy of the gospel. John took the trouble to find out that they had a primitive form of worship which was very like that in the New Hebrides.

Later John met an old Aboriginal woman who loved God and was a faithful servant of the Lord Jesus Christ. Her name was Nora Hood. She read her Bible and frequently spoke to her friends about her Saviour. She was also praying for the conversion of her husband. Nora, who lived in the camp in terrible conditions, said, 'Do not think that I like this miserable hut, or the food, or the company; but I am and have been happy in trying to do good amongst my people.'

When John visited her he found her reading her Bible and a church newspaper. He asked her a simple question: 'Nora, they tell me you are a Christian ... I hope that as a Christian you will speak the truth.' Nora was rather hurt that John should doubt her word. 'I am a Christian,' she replied. 'I fear and serve the true God. I always speak the truth.'

After some time together she and John wrote to each other, and in one of her letters she said: 'I am always reading my Bible, for I believe in God the Father and in Christ Jesus our Lord ... I always teach my children to pray to God our Father in heaven ... Sir, I shall always pray for you, that God may bless and guide you. O, Sir, pray for me, my husband, and my children!' In another letter she said, 'I hope you will go home to England safely, get more missionaries, and then go back to your poor blacks on the islands...'

Soon enough money had been given to build a new ship for the mission. It was built in Canada and named 'Dayspring'.

It was then suggested that John return to Scotland where he could visit churches and create an interest in missions generally, and the New Hebrides in particular. John really wanted to go back to the islands and continue his work there, but his friends encouraged him to go home.

John's missionary friends on Aneityum, Dr and Mrs Inglis, had just returned from Britain where they had been arranging for the New Testament to be printed in the language of the island people. They too encouraged John to go home.

After much prayer John decided to take their advice and on 16 May 1863 he sailed from Australia for Scotland on the ship, 'Kosciusko'. He had left home five years before and never thought that he would return. So much had happened to him during the time away.

John enjoyed the journey to England, especially because the ship's captain was a Christian. He invited John and a second minister on board to conduct worship services for the passengers and crew.

The time was mainly restful but one very exciting thing did happen. A violent thunderstorm struck as they sailed round the Cape of Good Hope. The ship was struck by lightning which caused it to plunge deeply in the waves, throwing passengers and crew about. Some people were knocked unconscious, and while no one was seriously hurt, John had his leg caught between his chair and the table at which he was sitting. It was badly bruised and he had to be carried to his cabin.

John led those on board in public prayer. He prayed, 'Let us thank the Lord for this most merciful deliverance. The ship is not on fire and no one is seriously injured!' The captain also gave John a souvenir; a piece of copper from the ship which had been melted and twisted by the lightning.

Australian Aborigines and bark shelter by Doris Meeson (1869-1955). Reproduced by permission of the National Library of Australia.

something to think about

1. John was very upset about the treatment of the Aborigines by the white people. Some believed the Aborigines were little better than animals and not worth teaching. Did John believe that everyone is important enough to hear the gospel? The Canaanite people in the Bible were also often seen as little more than animals and not worth bothering with.
Read Matthew 15:21-28 and see how gently Jesus speaks to the Canaanite woman.

2. Today in Australia the churches have a mission to the Aboriginal people, many of whom are now godly people. Try and find out more about them.

3. Did John want to go home to Scotland? Why was he encouraged to go and what did his friends want him to do while he was there?

26
Home to Scotland

Arriving in London he made his way to the train station and set off for Scotland to meet with the Missions' Committee of the Reformed Presbyterian Church. When a date was set for a further gathering of the committee, John set out for Torthorwald to meet his parents whom he had not seen for five years. During that time they must have wondered if they would ever see their missionary son again on this earth. When they met they praised God for his goodness in caring for each other, and bringing about this joyful reunion. Many tears were shed over the death of Mary and baby Peter.

All too soon John left for Coldstream to meet Mary's parents, who were still grieving the loss of their daughter. However, they accepted her death without complaining, and trusted in the wisdom of God's plan for everyone.

John visited as many churches and Sunday Schools as possible in Scotland, speaking about the mission work being carried out in the New Hebrides. Although the people did not have much themselves, they gave generously. Clothes and other gifts were given to the islanders and money was collected for the mission work. Appeals were also made for more missionaries.

As an act of honour, John was appointed the Moderator (Chairman) of his church. This was the highest honour that they could confer upon him.

In winter it is bitterly cold in northern Scotland. Snow and ice often cover most of the roads and travelling can be very unpleasant. On his trip to northern Scotland, from Wick to Thurso, the mail coach had no free seats inside, so John had to sit on an outside seat. He developed very bad frostbite to one foot but continued on his journey with no feeling in that foot.

Then came a trip by steamer to the Orkney Isles during rough weather. John asked to be allowed to remain on deck as he disliked the smoke fumes from the engine and people drinking and smoking.

At first the captain said, 'No! You'll be washed overboard!' However, he finally agreed, having some crew members cover him with a tarpaulin, and tying it to the mast. Reaching his destination John found his frostbitten foot to be still numb, and painful when he walked. He could only manage to hold two meetings and had to cancel the rest. A visit to a doctor resulted in a plaster cast being put on the injured foot. Part of his foot had died due to frostbite but with more treatment John was able to walk. However, for the rest of his life he had pain in that foot.

During his time in Scotland John met Margaret Whitecross, a fine Christian lady, who, with her family, had a great interest in mission work. As a result John and Margaret were married in Edinburgh in 1864.

All too soon it was time to return to Australia and then to the mission field. The newly married couple spent time meeting friends and relations, saying farewell. At Torthorwald they bowed in prayer, and when they left John's mother kept back her tears until the couple disappeared out of sight.

In October, 1864 John and Margaret made their way to Liverpool where they boarded a ship named 'Crest of the Wave' and they settled down to the journey to Australia. The men and women who had volunteered for mission work in the New Hebrides stayed in Australia to do some medical training. John remembered how vital his own medical experience had been and wanted all the missionaries to have similar training. This would prove valuable when working with the natives.

They arrived in Sydney on 17 January 1865 and discovered that their two masted ship, 'Dayspring' was in dock. However, no money was available to pay the crew and this was causing a stir. John took £50 out of his pocket, gave it to the men and set about getting the additional money needed to pay the crew in full. As he looked at the ship he remembered all the small amounts of money given by the Sunday school children. He told himself, 'The Lord has provided – the Lord will provide.'

Nobody seemed able to help John find the money to pay the crew. Some ministers even suggested the 'Dayspring' be sold. John argued that since many Sunday schools had given money for the building of the ship, then surely the churches in Australia could give the money needed to keep her working. The annual salary for a crew was just £120.

John spoke at the morning service in Sydney, explaining the mission's need. In the afternoon he spoke at a small mission hall near the harbour. After the service he was approached by the captain of a ship berthed near the 'Dayspring'. 'My wife and I, being too late to get on shore to attend any church in the city, heard this little chapel bell ringing, and followed when we saw you going up the hill. We have so enjoyed the service... This cheque for £50 will be a beginning to help you out of your difficulties.'

At a later worship service, when the congregation heard of the need of money, one man stood up and said, 'I'll give you £10.' Another said, 'I shall send you £20 tomorrow morning.'

Soon money was coming through the post and John and his friends were able to praise God and give him thanks for opening the wallets of the Australian Christians to support the mission.

something to think about

1. What was the attitude of Mary's parents to the death of their daughter?
   Read Philippians 1:21. When the Apostle Paul said 'to die is gain', he knew that when he died he was going to ... and that he was going to be with ...

2. In Australia some people were very generous with their money.
   Proverbs 22:9 tells us what will happen to a generous man (or person). What is it?

3. Where was John living when he had his medical training? You will find the answer somewhere in chapter 8. Do you think he found the training useful?

27
A British warship calls at Tanna

In May 1865 John and Margaret and Bob, their newly born son, set sail on the 'Dayspring' for the New Hebrides where John trusted he and Margaret could return to Tanna.

Arriving at Aneityum, John prayed that they would be directed to move to Tanna, but they were asked to return to return to Australia and make undertake a tour collecting offerings for the mission. A committee would be responsible for the collection and banking of the giving. This would ensure the financial stability of the mission and the 'Dayspring'.

After sailing about the islands of the New Hebrides, showing Mary the islands and meeting local Christian workers, preparations were made to leave for Australia. However, during the time John and Margaret were in the New Hebrides, they were visited by a British warship, the 'HMS Curaçoa' commanded by Commodore Sir William Wiseman.

The ship had called to deal with the murder of the British missionaries, George and Ellen Gordon, on the island of Erromanga, and the violence against John and others on the island of Tanna. As the native language was unknown to the Commodore, John was asked to come on board and act as an interpreter. The warship called at each island warning the natives to respect the missionaries, as violence would not be tolerated by the British.

'No one is trying to force you to become Christians,' the Commodore told them. 'You encouraged white people to come and live among you and you sold them land and promised to protect them. But instead of keeping those promises, you have killed some of them and tried to kill others. You stole or destroyed their property.'

The Captain warned the natives that such behaviour had to end. He also told them that Queen Victoria would send a war ship to call in each year to make sure the natives treated the missionaries with kindness. He also said he would investigate any complaints they made against cruelty by Europeans.

When the 'Curaçoa' reached Tanna, three days were spent investigating events that had taken place. The captain said if the natives would not co-operate and point out those responsible for the killings and destruction, he would destroy at least two villages with the ship's canons. As Chief Nowar had attempted to aid John, he was told that his villages would be spared. By saying this the captain was frightening the natives in an effort to make sure they respected the missionaries – their work and property.

The inhabitants of the two villages escaped to Chief Nowar's lands, but before the appointed time for the Curaçoa's guns to open fire, a large group of Tannese warriors armed and painted for battle appeared on the beach, announcing that they were going to destroy the war ship.

When John saw the sailors preparing to open fire he went to the commodore and with tears in his eyes, begged, 'Surely you are not going to shell these poor and foolish Tannese?'

However the captain rebuked John saying, 'You are here as interpreter, not as my adviser. If I leave without punishing them now, no vessel or white man will be safe at this harbour. You can go on board your own ship, till I require your services again.'

When the command was given, 'Fire!' The native warriors, who were performing their war dance, turned and ran for their lives.

The exploding shells threw large lumps of earth into the sky as the natives disappeared over the hill and made their way to the safety of Chief Nowar's territory. Turning the canons towards the two villages the command was given to fire, and soon most of the houses were destroyed. A party of well armed sailors went ashore to complete the work of destruction.

No natives were killed in the gunfire, although one died when he began to take the metal from an unexploded shell which suddenly blew up. One sailor was also shot when he wandered away from his companions, entered a native plantation and began munching on a stick of sugar-cane.

When John reached Sydney, he found the newspapers filled with news of what was said to be a crime against the poor native people of Tanna. John was even being blamed for taking part in the killing of the natives, and with the sailors on the 'Dayspring', had cheered when they saw what was being done. It was also incorrectly reported that many piles of dead native bodies were soon collected on the shore.

John told the newspapers his side of the story and threatened legal action if they didn't report the truth and apologise for their incorrect statements. He also appealed to Commodore Sir William Wiseman to support his version of the incident. John knew that his conscience was clear before the Lord and that he had not done anything to be ashamed of. Later when an enquiry was held, John and the others were not held responsible.

Despite wanting to get back to the New Hebrides as soon as possible, John again began a speaking tour of Australia seeking support for missionaries and the 'Dayspring'.

It was during that time that John's position as a missionary from his church in Scotland ended, and he was accepted as a missionary from the Australian Presbyterian churches. Returning to the New Hebrides, John and Margaret were longing to return to Tanna, but after discussions and prayer is was agreed that they would commence a gospel work on the island of Aniwa. John knew they needed the gospel as much as did the people of Tanna.

something to think about

1. John prayed that he and Margaret would go straight back to Tanna but God had other plans for them and they went to Australia. Why were they asked to go there?

2. Our plans are not always the same as God's plans.
   Read Jonah 1:1-3:5. This is a long reading. Here we are told that Jonah disobeyed God when he told him to go to Nineveh. What happened to Jonah when he went against God's plan and did Jonah eventually do what God wanted?

3. Why did John have to act as an interpreter to Sir William Wiseman?

4. Why was Chief Nowar told that his villages would be spared from the ship's cannons?

28
Aniwa!

Before setting out for Aniwa a conference was held. The 'Dayspring' was used to collect missionaries and give them the opportunity to visit the many islands in the New Hebrides.

After the conference the ship was called to the aid of the 'John Williams', the vessel used by the members of the London Missionary Society, which had become stuck on a coral reef. During their stay at Aneityum John was told of the death of his old Christian friend, Abraham. He had given his watch to a friend asking him to give it to John: 'Give it to Missi, my own Missi Paton,' Abraham said, 'and tell him that I go to Jesus, where time is dead.'

John also was saddened to learn of the death of his faithful dog, Clutha, who had pined away after his escape from Tanna.

At last the day came for the missionaries to take up their posts. On 8 August 1866 the 'Dayspring' set sail with a number of missionaries ready to take up their work. John and Margaret were overjoyed to be travelling with John's old friend, Joseph Copeland and his wife, Elizabeth.

When the natives saw the ship call at their island and unload missionaries and all their possessions, they found it difficult to understand why they should come back. The missionaries were not returning to make money out of trading but simply to tell them the good news concerning God and his Son, the Lord Jesus Christ. They asked one another, 'We killed or drove them all away! We plundered their houses and robbed them. Had we been so treated, nothing would have made us return. But they come back with a beautiful new ship and with more and more missionaries!' Some began to think, 'If their God makes them do that then maybe we should worship him also.'

On their way to Aniwa they called at Tanna, where Chief Nowar pleaded with John to return to the island. He promised him total protection, food and whatever was needed. He spoke to Margaret and pleaded with her to have John take up his old work on Tanna. However, this was not to be and in November, 1866 they set foot on Aniwa, an island about seven miles long and two miles in width. There was no harbour, just a gap in the coral reef surrounding the island. The dock was made of several big coral boulders rolled together in one spot, but in rough weather is was impossible to load and unload cargo.

The island was a beautiful place, where the sun shone brightly most days of the year. The ocean swell broke on the shore, creating a sound that could be heard all over the island. The highest place on the island was about one hundred metres above sea level. As there were no mountains, clouds did not form, and so there was usually a continual shortage of fresh drinking water. There was however, no shortage of lush trees and plenty of delicious fruit.

John and Margaret were greeted by the quiet, unsmiling natives, but soon Margaret was taken by the hand and led across the coral reef to the shore. It was Kanathie, the wife of a Christian worker from Aneityum, who had taken her hand.

Most of the natives did not wear clothes, but the married women and older ladies wore grass skirts. The natives were very interested to see what John and Margaret had brought with them. They were particularly interested in the hooks, axes, knives, rolls of calico and the blankets. Margaret thought the scene so funny when John began to hand out gifts, that she had to get out of the building where they were, and laugh outside. One man left the hut wearing just a white vest, while another wore a dress pinned around his throat. His fingers could be seen poking out under the hem. A third native used a native bag as a hat.

John and Margaret made their home in a native hut which had been prepared for them. This hut had just one big room which was used for worship each Sunday. It had no windows or doors, just spaces left where they would have been. The walls were made from sugar cane leaves and reeds woven together over a wooden frame. A thatched roof kept out the rain. The floor was made of broken pieces of white coral mixed with the dirt. One end was screened off, and that was the bedroom. John and Margaret packed all their possessions in boxes at the other end.

Margaret cooked outside, usually with many natives watching. They ate their meals using boxes as chairs and a box lid as the table.

When the time came for the building of their own home, John asked if he could buy land on high ground. The natives refused, but sold him land a quarter of a mile from his first choice. When he began clearing the site, many natives watched, hoping their gods would strike him dead.

One day John pointed to the box of human bones he had collected on his land, and asked Chief Namakei, 'Where did these bones come from?' Shrugging his shoulders the chief replied, 'Ah, we are not Tanna men! We don't eat the bones!'

Some time later John discovered why the natives had insisted he buy that particular piece of land: 'When Missi came we saw his boxes. We knew he had blankets and calico, axes and knives, fishhooks and all such things. We said, "Don't drive him off, else we will lose all these things. We will let him land. But we will force him to live on the sacred plot. Our gods will kill him, and we will divide all that he has amongst the men of Aniwa."'

The chief continued, 'But, Missi built his house on our most sacred spot. He and his people lived there, and the gods did not strike him down. He planted bananas there, and we said, "Now when they eat those bananas they will all drop down dead, as our fathers assured. Only our sacred men could do that." These bananas ripened. They did eat them. We kept watching for days and days, but no one died! Therefore what can we say? Our fathers told us things that were not true. Our gods cannot kill them. Their Jehovah God is stronger than the gods of Aniwa.'

So it was that God used the piece of land to make the natives question their gods.

The first 'Dayspring'

Margaret Paton loved sketching. This shows a volcano on Tanna.

something to think about

1. What message did Abraham leave for John when he died?

2. Why did the natives want John to have his house built on a particular piece of land?

3. **Read 1 Kings 18:22-40**. This is a long reading but in verse 27 what are the four things that Elijah said the false gods may be doing? He is making fun of the false gods.
    False gods can do absolutely nothing for they have no power at all. The missionaries ate the bananas grown on a 'sacred spot' and nothing happened to them.
    So what did God use to make the natives question their gods?

29
Work commences

While John worked on the new house, Margaret stayed in their native hut with little Bob. One day she heard a rustling sound behind the boxes. She was about to carefully and quietly lift the curtain when in the gloom she saw a pair of eyes staring at her. The small man threw back the curtain and shouted angrily, 'Why are you looking at me?'

'Because I did not know who was there,' Margaret replied.

The man did not believe her and shouted back, 'You plenty lie! You 'fraid me steal. Me no steal! Me come to worship. Why did you think I steal?'

The man left, only to return with about twenty of his friends who sat outside the house watching, while the little native, holding his club, said again and again, 'You plenty lie!'

After several hours of this Margaret picked up little Bobby and carefully made her way to the pathway leading to John. When she had passed the natives she began to run and was soon safe with her husband. Margaret was afraid of what had happened but little Bobby thought the run was really exciting.

The natives of Aniwa were less troublesome than the Tannese. They didn't cause the same trouble stealing the missionaries' possessions, and the news of the Curaçao's visit to Tanna, with the terrifying demonstration of the destruction that her cannons could cause, meant the local natives were careful how they treated John and Margaret. They didn't want to face the angry cannons of a British warship.

The people of Aniwa were once at war with the people of Aneityum. Some natives from Aniwa had visited Aneityum, before any missionaries were in the area. There all but two were killed and eaten. When the ones who had escaped made their way home to Aniwa and told of the killings, revenge was demanded. However, the islands were forty eight miles apart and to send an invading party was almost impossible. To keep the hatred alive, each year the warriors of Aniwa added to a trench they had commenced digging. They lengthened the trench by a metre each year and added a branch from a nearby tree to the pile that was already there. In this way the hatred was kept alive for almost eighty years.

One day two Christian natives came from Aneityum to Aniwa, where they were promised protection from the local natives. The senior island chief, Namakei, was faithful to his word, even when it was discovered they came from the tribe that had long before killed his people. In order to take revenge and at the same time make sure none of the locals killed them, Chief Namakei hired three warriors to come over from Tanna island and carry out the killing. One of the three men had recently lost his son and blamed the missionaries for his death.

One Sunday evening as the native missionaries were returning from a worship service in a village, they were attacked. One was killed and the other, Navalak, badly wounded.

Chief Namakei nursed the injured man back to health and told the natives that their honour had been satisfied with the death of the one missionary. Navalak returned to his own village in peace.

Some time later the chief sent word to Aneityum that the feud was ended and teachers would now be welcomed in Aniwa. The local natives were not interested in the Christian gospel, but this would encourage trading ships to call at the island and they would be able to buy knives, axes, blankets and guns. Two new native Christians and their wives were sent to the island –

and it was one of these who, on their arrival, had helped Margaret across the coral reef to the shore.

With other helpers from Aneityum, John's building program was well under way. However, he slipped while using his axe and badly cut his ankle. Not being able to work and tell the natives what was to be done, they were returned to Aneityum. The local natives were not interested in work, even when offered payment of fishhooks and other pieces of equipment. The men of Aniwa usually stood around and watched their womenfolk do the work.

The work was continued when John's foot improved, and soon a well built home was on his piece of land. It was built above ground level to allow the cool breezes to flow about and under the house, which kept it cool in the hot weather. The wide verandahs also provided much shade.

At first there were two main rooms but later additions of a pantry, bathhouse, and storage rooms, gave them six rooms in all. When hurricanes or cyclones struck the island they would squeeze into the cellar where it was safe, while outside trees and buildings were torn apart and blown everywhere.

Over the years a little village grew up on the mission land. There were two small homes for orphans – one for boys and the other for girls. They had a hut for worship and another for the school, and eventually John had a carpenter's workshop and space for a blacksmith to work. Many trees provided shade and a constant supply of food for everyone. This included coconuts and many different kinds of fruit.

Soon many natives set to work copying John's building to rebuild their own homes. And all the time John and Margaret were learning the language of the local people. Every day after lunch, a bell was rung to let the islanders know that John was available to give advice and medicines if needed. All who came to speak with John were given a cup of tea and a piece of bread prepared by Margaret.

something to think about

1. There was war between the people who lived on Aniwa and the people who lived on Aneityum. This resulted in grudges being kept. What did the natives do to keep the grudge alive in their minds and what should our attitude be toward those who hurt us?
   Read Matthew 5:38-42. Do we always have this attitude?

2. Why were the natives better behaved now and of what were they afraid?

3. In this chapter we see how helpful John and Margaret were to the people. This included providing homes for boys and girls who were orphaned. Can you find what other help they gave and what Margaret always offered to those who came to see them?

30
Exciting days

Both John and Margaret continued learning the language of the local natives. Every time they heard a new word it was written down in English. This was done as John looked forward to the day when the people could read the Scriptures in their own language.

One day while building the new house, John realised that he needed more nails and some tools. Picking up a flat piece of wood he wrote down a message for Margaret, asking her to send the equipment he needed.

Chief Namakei took the piece of timber and asked, 'But what do you want?'

'The wood will tell her,' John replied.

The chief walked off with a strange look on his face and saying, 'Whoever heard of wood speaking?'

When he handed the wood to Margaret he was surprised to see her take some nails and tools and hand them to him – the very things that John had said he wanted. John explained to Chief Namakei about reading, and the need of the natives to be able to read their language when it was in written form. He also showed the chief the Bible and said that one day when the people could read they would be able to hear God speaking to them from the pages of Scripture.

A chief from an inland village visited John with his three sons but after they returned home, one son fell ill. He blamed the missionaries and threatened to kill John and his companions if the boy died. However, John treated the sick son, and prayed that God would intervene and spare the boy's life. When the boy recovered the chief helped John in every way he could. He attended the worship and assisted John by translating his words to the local people.

When two rooms in the house were completed, John hired two natives to carry his possessions to the new building. They carried the heavy packages suspended from a pole resting on their shoulders. Soon afterwards one of the two men fell ill and died and the blame was placed again on the missionaries. The warning was given that if the second man died, so also would John. Again God stepped in and the man lived.

To get goods from the landing wharf to the new house, John made a wheelbarrow and paid the natives to build a road sealed with coral. This was a much safer and easier way for the men to move the boxes.

Not all natives welcomed the missionaries. Often there were threats to kill them all and burn their buildings. On one occasion a warrior from Erromanga began to follow John, armed with a club and a musket. John sent for a local chief and told him if any missionary was harmed, Jehovah would hold him responsible.

The chief said that he knew nothing about the man's evil plans. 'Missi,' he said, 'I did not know. I did not know. But by the first favourable wind he shall go, and you will see him no more.' The chief did as he said.

Sometimes, when an angry native appeared, John would stare him in the eyes and grab his arms. The natives rarely did any harm to someone who was looking at them. John would tightly hold the person until the anger disappeared.

Chief Namakei, who owned the land surrounding the mission building, enjoyed visiting John and Margaret. He was always given a drink of tea and a piece of bread. The first time he was followed by many of his people who watched what happened. Before the chief had his cup of tea he handed it around for his people to taste.

Before long he was visiting the mission complex with his friend, Chief Naswai and his wife Katua. These three were amongst the first to openly confess their love of God and faith in the Lord Jesus Christ.

Chief Namakei didn't have a son, only a daughter, and when Margaret gave birth to a son, whom they called Fred, he wanted to name him as his heir. He brought people to see little Fred, saying, 'Look at the white chief of Aniwa.' When Fred could walk, the chief led him around to meet all the people, and it wasn't long before he could fluently speak the chief's language. The close friendship that grew between Chief Namakei and little Fred helped win the friendship of all the natives on the island.

It was the birth to John and Margaret of a daughter they named Minn that resulted in a change in attitude of the people to baby girls. The native woman expected Margaret and John to be upset at the birth of a daughter, but when they saw how little Minn was loved by her parents they went away very excited because they had seen 'a real little white woman of Aniwa.'

'All little girls of Aniwa will be more lovingly treated in the days to come, for the love we showed to this 'Little Woman of Aniwa', Margaret said.

Before long Chief Namakei brought his daughter Litsi to the missionaries saying, 'I want to leave my Litsi with you. I want you to train her for Jesus.' She proved a real help to Margaret and before long her uncle Kalangi brought his daughter to Margaret to be trained like her cousin. When the children returned to their homes they spoke of Jesus which proved a valuable way of spreading the gospel story.

These two girls were the first of many who came to the missionaries to be taught the skills of Europe and the truth concerning the Lord Jesus Christ.

something to think about

1. Why did John want the natives to have a written language of their own? What was the first step in giving them their own written language?

2. What did Chief Namakei think of little Fred?

3. How do you think the birth of little Minn helped the future little girls of Aniwa?
   Read Matthew 19:13-15. Here we see Jesus blessing the children. Why do you think the Bible tell us that Jesus loves all children, both boys and girls?

31
A wedding on Aniwa

One morning a native named Tupa ran to the house and called out excitedly, 'Missi, I have killed the Tebil! I have killed Teapolo. He came to catch me last night. I raised all the people and we fought him round the house with our clubs. At daybreak he came out and I killed him dead. We will have no more bad conduct or trouble now. Teapolo is dead!' John knew that 'Teapolo' was their word for 'devil', so he answered, 'What nonsense! Teapolo is a spirit and cannot be seen.'

When the man insisted that he really had killed the 'Teapolo,' Margaret suggested that John should go and see what he was talking about. The man led John to a lump of sacred coral, and showed him the body of a huge sea-serpent. 'There he lies!' said Tupa. 'Truly I killed him.'

'That is not the devil,' John told him. 'It is only the body of a serpent.'

'Well, but it is all the same!' Tupa answered at once. 'He is Teapolo. He makes us bad and causes all our troubles.'

As God worked in the hearts of the natives they began to give up their cruel ways. No more were children killed by angry fathers and no more were wives killed because they did not agree with their husbands. When Chief Namakei and Chief Naswai became Christians they told their people, 'We are the men of Christ now. We must not fight. We must put down murders and crimes among our people.'

Some natives wanted to kill John and drive the missionaries away from Aniwa. Pavingin was a sacred man who had been on Tanna when the 'Dayspring' called with the missionaries on board. He explained that Chief Nowar had given him his bracelet and made him promise to protect 'Missi' from harm. If he failed the men of Tanna would come and punish them! That ended the talk of murder – it was decided to leave 'Missi' alone.

On another occasion John noticed a man with a tomahawk in his hand, hanging around. Feeling a little ill at ease John asked, 'Nelwang, do you want to speak to me?'

'Yes, Missi,' he replied. 'If you will help me now, I will be your friend for ever.'

John asked, 'Well, how can I help you?'

To this Nelwang replied, 'I want to get married and I need your help.'

Nelwang explained that he wanted to marry Yakin, who was the widow of a chief who had died, and was therefore free to marry again.

John asked, 'Do you know if she loves you?'

'Yes,' replied Nelwang. 'One day I met her on the path and told her I would like to have her for my wife. She took out her earrings and gave them to me... I was one of her husband's men, and if she had loved any of them more than she loved me, she would have given them to another. With the earrings she gave me her heart.'

'Then why,' asked John, 'don't you go and marry her?'

Nelwang explained the problem: 'In her village there are thirty young men for whom there are no wives. Each of them wants her but no one has the courage to take her, for the other twenty-nine will shoot him!' He knew that if he tried to marry her, all thirty warriors would turn on him and kill him. He asked John what he would do, if he were in Nelwang's place.

John suggested that they should elope! With the help of a couple of his friends, who were sworn to secrecy, Nelwang, in the dead of night, broke through the fence surrounding Yakin's house and carried her off into the bush to marry her.

When the other warriors discovered what had taken place they were very angry. They broke down the fences around both Nelwang and Yakin's houses and began destroying their property. After this had gone on for a couple of days John appeared on the scene while the men were feasting on Nelwang's crops.

He asked Chief Naswai, 'What's this your men are doing?'

The chief explained: 'Nelwang has eloped with Yakin.'

'Oh,' said John, 'is that all? Call your men and let me speak to them.'

Turning to the young men he said, 'After all your kindness to Yakin, has she really run away and left you all? You should be thankful that you are free from such an ungrateful woman? Are you really making all this noise over such a person?' Soon the warriors agreed that Yakin was not worth the trouble, and that Nelwang would be sufficiently punished by having such a woman as his wife!

Some weeks later, during which time nothing had been heard from the runaways, Nelwang found John when he was working by himself and told him, 'I come now to do as I promised: I will help you, and Yakin will help Missi Paton, and we shall be your friends.'

Nelwang asked if he and his bride could come and stay at the mission house for several days while all the anger died down and a house was ready for them. John agreed to this. Yakin was a great help around the house to Margaret and a fearful Nelwang followed John around like a shadow. They both showed a real interest in the gospel and when converted, Yakin became a Sunday school teacher and led the singing when Margaret was unable to do so.

The day came for the newly married couple to appear in public and John encouraged them to do this at the worship service. The bell announcing worship stopped ringing and everyone sat down. Nelwang entered at the very last moment smartly dressed in a shirt and kilt, but carrying his tomahawk in case there was trouble. He sat as close to John as he could.

Then in walked Yakin. It was the custom for natives to begin wearing clothes if they were converted and she had put on every piece of clothing she had! Over her grass skirt she wore a man's overcoat which reached down to her ankles. On top of that she wore a vest, and her head and shoulders stuck out from the seat of a pair of man's trousers, with the two empty trouser-legs dangling down either side in front of her. She had a red shirt fastened to one shoulder and a striped one to the other. These flapped like wings as she walked along. Another red shirt was around her head like a turban, with a sleeve hanging down over each ear. The sight of her sitting sweltering in the heat under the weight of all those clothes made John keep the service as short as he could. He said it was probably the shortest service he had ever conducted in his life!

Nelwang, however, smiled lovingly at his beautiful wife and gave John a proud look as if to say, 'You never saw such a lovely bride!'

A typical native
Christian teacher

Mission house on Aniwa

something to think about

1. John may have had very good motives for saying that Yakin
    was an ungrateful woman but it was not really true. Why
    do you think he said what he did and how did it help
    Nelwang and Yakin?
    Abraham was called 'God's friend' **(read James 2:23)** but
    even he was not entirely truthful when he said twice that
    Sarah was his sister instead of his wife - **read Genesis
    12:11-13 and Genesis 20:2.**
    This shows us that even Christians can sometimes do things
    that go against God's law **(read Exodus 20:16)** even though
    they may have very good reasons for doing so.

2. Describe Nelwang and Yakin as they appeared at the
    worship service after their marriage. Although they must have
    looked strange we must not laugh at them but try to
    understand why they dressed as they did. Why do you think
    that was?

32
God's special 'rain'

Fresh water, on the island of Aniwa, was always in short supply as very little rain fell during the year. The wet season was usually December to April, but when John began to fill his two large water barrels from the local water hole he was stopped as the natives believed there would be none left for them. He was soon to learn that the water supply was controlled by the sacred men. The islanders had to bring them presents to make it rain. If the rain failed to fall the sacred men blamed the tribes people and demanded bigger presents. They had real power over them.

The lack of water did not worry the islanders too much as they drank coconut juice (which looked and tasted a little like lemonade) and chewed sugar cane when they were thirsty. They washed themselves and their clothes in the sea. However they did need water for cooking.

John decided that he would dig a well. He had dug a successful well on the island of Tanna and prayed to God that he would guide him to dig in the right spot on Aniwa. One day he called Chief Namakei and Chief Naswai, and told them of his plan: 'I am going to dig a deep well into the ground, to see if our God will send us fresh water up from below.'

The men looked at him as if he was mad. 'O Missi!' one of them said, 'Rain comes only from above. How could you expect our island to send up showers of rain from below?'

When John tried to explain that fresh water did spring up out of the ground in his own country, they told him, 'O Missi, your head is going wrong, or you would not talk like that! Don't let our people hear you talking about going down into the earth for rain, or they will never listen to you or believe you again!' However, John started digging with the help of some of young natives who helped empty the buckets of earth.

The following morning John found that the walls of the well had fallen in. None of the natives were willing to go near the well, fearing that John was mad and there would be the loss of life if the walls fell in while anyone was in the well.

The old chief came to John and pleaded with him to give up his scheme: 'Now, had you been in that hole last night you would have been buried, and a man-of-war would have come from Queen 'Toria to ask for the Missi who lived here. We would have to say, "He is down in that hole." The captain would have asked, "Who killed him and put him down there? Whoever heard of a white man going down into the earth to bury himself? You killed him, you put him down there!" Then he would bring out his big guns and shoot us and destroy our island in revenge. You are digging your own grave, Missi, and you will dig ours too… Please give it up now?'

But John worked on. He rigged up a pulley and when he had filled the bucket with earth he rang a little bell and the natives pulled it to the top. After emptying it they lowered it again to John.

When the well was about ten metres deep John, after much prayer, announced, 'I think that Jehovah God will give us water tomorrow from that hole.'

Still the chief was sure it wouldn't work. 'No, Missi,' he said, 'you will never see rain coming up from the earth on this island. We think that if you reach water, we will see you drop through into the sea, and the sharks will eat you! That will be the end of it – death to you and danger to us.' But John told him, 'Come tomorrow. I hope and believe that Jehovah God will send you the rainwater up through the earth.'

John really believed that the Lord would answer his prayer. The next morning he and others made their way to the well. When he lowered himself to the bottom of the well he dug a small hole in the centre and there he saw a small bubble of fresh water. John jumped for joy as he tasted the sweet spring water.

Waiting for the dirt in the water to settle, John took a jug full and sent it to the natives at the mouth of the well. The old chief took the jug, tasted the water, and joyfully exclaimed, 'Rain! Rain! Yes, it's rain! But how did you get it?'

John gave all the thanks to Jehovah, his God: 'Jehovah, my God gave it out of his own earth in answer to our prayers and work. Go and watch it springing up through the ground!'

Making a line and joining hands, one by one the natives leaned over the well and watched as the spring water bubbled into the well. When one saw the water he ran to the end of the line and linked arms to support the next native who gazed down. The next job was to shore up the side of the well, which was done with large blocks of coral that had been washed up on the during cyclones. With the bucket and winding gear in place water was readily available. God had answered the prayer of his believing servant.

The chief then turned to John and exclaimed, 'Missi, wonderful, wonderful is the work of your Jehovah God! No god of Aniwa ever helped us in this way.'

The men were full of questions: 'Will it always rain up through the earth, or will it come and go like the rain from the clouds? … Will you or your family drink it all, or shall we also have some?' When John told them he was sure there would always be plenty for all of them, they could hardly believe it: 'Then, it will be our water and we may all use it as our very own?'

John said that the water would always be there for their use, as a good gift from God. 'You and all of your people,' he assured the chief, 'may come and drink and carry away as much of it as you wish, and the more of it we can use the fresher it will be. That is the way with many of our Jehovah's best gifts to men, and for it … we praise his name!'

The natives were afraid that if anything bad happened to John, the H.M.S. Cordelia, sent by Queen Victoria, would come with their big guns and destroy them. This picture shows John greeting Captain Vernon of the Cordelia.

Each in turn had a look down the well while
the others held on to him from behind.

something to think about

1. What did the people of Aniwa think would happen to them if John was hurt while digging the well?

2. What part did God play in this incident and what does it tell us about our God?

3. In the Bible water from a well is often called 'living water' and is used to symbolize eternal life. **Read John 4:7-26.** What does Jesus say to the woman in verse **13?**
   Do you think that those who drank from John's well on Aniwa would ever be thirsty again?

33
A fine sermon

Now that the well was being used, Chief Namakei asked John, 'Missi, I think I could help you next Sabbath. Will you let me preach a sermon about the well?' John agreed and the next Lord's Day a very large crowd turned up for the worship service. After John had prayed he asked the chief to deliver the sermon. He stood up, tomahawk in his hand, and began to glorify God, swinging the tomahawk when he wanted to stress what he was saying.

'Friends of Namakei,' he began, 'men and women and children of Aniwa, listen to me. Since Missi came here he has talked many strange things we could not understand – things all too wonderful; and we said that many of them must be lies ... But of all his wonderful stories, we thought the strangest was about digging down through the earth to get rain!'

He reminded them how they had thought John was mad when he told them his God would give him rain from the earth. 'We mocked him,' Namakei went on, 'but the water was there all the same. We have laughed at other things which the Missi told us, because we could not see them. But from this day I believe that all he tells us about his Jehovah God is true! Some day our eyes will see it, for today we have seen the rain from the ground.'

If they had not seen it with their own eyes, nothing in the world, Namakei continued, would have made them believe that rain could come from the depths of the earth.

Then, thumping his chest as he spoke, he went on to tell his hearers: 'Something here in my heart tells me that Jehovah God does exist, the Invisible One, of whom we never heard nor saw till the Missi brought him to our knowledge.'

Just as the water had been there all the time, though their eyes could not see it, he declared, so I, your chief, do now firmly believe that when I die... I shall... see the invisible Jehovah God with my soul, as Missi tells me, as surely as I have seen the rain from the earth below. From this day, my people, I must worship the God who has opened for us the well and who fills it with rain from below. The gods of Aniwa cannot hear and cannot help us like the God of Missi. Henceforth I am a follower of Jehovah God!' He then urged everyone to get the idols that their fathers had worshipped and bring them to John to be burnt and destroyed, once and for all.

He continued 'Let us be taught by the Missi how to serve the God who can hear, the Jehovah who gave us the well and who will give us every other blessing, for he sent his Son Jesus to die for us and bring us to heaven...' He concluded by saying, 'Jehovah God has sent us rain from the earth. Why should he not also send us his Son from heaven? Namakei stands up for Jehovah!'

That afternoon many idols were burned, buried or thrown out to sea. Soon almost every home thanked God for giving them their daily food and most conducted some family worship. People began to look forward to the worship on the Lord's Day. Many cooked their Sunday meals on Saturday in order to have more time for worship and to be taught about God by the missionaries.

People were no longer worried about their possessions being stolen so they gave up bringing their animals to worship. Laws were introduced with fines for anyone who stole another's possessions. The sacred men of the island gave up their old superstitious ways and made themselves responsible for making sure that the islanders kept God's law.

John, Margaret and the other Christians on the island praised and gave thanks to God for the wonderful change that had taken place in the lives of these people who had once been cannibals.

The chief and teachers of Aniwa

something to think about

1. Namakei preached a great sermon. What did he urge the people of Aniwa to do?

2. What effect did it have upon the natives?

3. Idols are often talked about in the Bible and we are always warned to keep away from them. **Read Exodus 20:4-6 and 1 John 5:21.**
Idols are often thought of as statues, carvings etc. which are found in big churches and are worshipped instead of God. But many other things can also be idols. It may be football or a footballer, athletics or an athlete or even pop music or a pop star; in fact anything that takes the place of God as centre of our lives.
Do you have any idols in your life? If so, you know what to do about them – for after all, they are only things of the world.

34.
I can see!

A successful well and Chief Namakei's sermon marked a turning point in the spiritual life of the people of Aniwa. Everyone was talking about God's rain from the ground. John had also printed portions of the Scriptures and some hymns.

Chief Namakei helped John, and when the pages began to mount up, he asked, 'Missi, is it done? Can it speak?' When John announced that the pages could speak, he read the words in the language of the natives. Again the chief was overjoyed to know it spoke his language.

However, Namakei couldn't get the page to speak for him. He was puzzled. At last, he handed it back to John saying, very sadly, 'Missi, I cannot make it speak! It will never speak to me!'

'No,' John explained. 'You don't know how to read it yet, how to make it speak to you; but I will teach you to read, and then it will speak to you as it does to me.'

Namakei could not wait to learn. 'O Missi, dear Missi, show me how to make it speak!' he begged.

John realised that Namakei had eyesight problems, so he searched through a collection of spectacles he had brought with him. At first the chief was fearful of wearing them, but when they were in place he shouted, 'I see it all now! This is what you told us about Jesus. He opened the eyes of a blind man. The word of Jesus has just come to Aniwa. He has sent me these glass eyes! I have my sight again, the sight that I had when a boy. O Missi, make the book speak to me now!'

At once John began to teach him the letters of the alphabet. Before long he was learning whole words. As John read from the book, Namakei was able to learn the passages by heart. He then encouraged the younger people to learn to read, saying, 'If an old man like me has done it, it should be much easier for you!'

Chief Namakei's wife, Yauwaki, was afraid of the missionaries and their worship, but one day coming quietly to the mission house, she looked in and saw Margaret playing her small organ and singing songs in the Aniwan language. Yauwaki, turned and ran, calling the women and girls to come to the mission house where they would 'hear the box sing!' After this the women and children flocked to Margaret to hear 'the box that sang' and Margaret at prayer.

One day Namakei approached John with a request: 'Missi, can you give my wife also a pair of new glass eyes like mine? She tries to learn, but she cannot see the letters. She tries to sew, but she pricks her finger and throws away the needle, saying, "The ways of the white people are not good!" If she could get a pair of glass eyes, she would be in a new world like Namakei.'

John looked in his box and found a pair of glasses for Yauwaki. She was scared of putting them on, but when at last she did, she was thrilled: 'Oh, my new eyes! my new eyes!' she exclaimed. 'I have the sight of a little girl. I will learn hard now. I will make up for lost time.' Although she was never very good at reading or sewing Yauwaki gave Margaret much help in teaching the younger people in the school.

The day came when an important decision was made by John – the time had come for the building of a place for worship. He encouraged the natives to become involved because of their love for Jesus. After lengthy discussion and speeches the work commenced, the men preparing the timber and the women getting the sugar cane leaves for the thatched roof. The floor was covered with pieces of white coral, on which mats were placed for the congregation.

The new building was no sooner constructed than a hurricane struck the island and destroyed the it. The people were greatly upset but John encouraged them saying, 'Let us not weep, like boys over their broken bows and arrows! Let us be strong and build a yet stronger church for Jehovah.'

When they ran out of long beams for the roof, a chief who was opposed to the first building appeared with some of his people, carrying a long pole for the centre of the roof. He was singing, dancing and beating time with his tomahawk as his men carried the beam. It had come out of his hut and was covered with soot, but it was just what was needed for the church building.

Coral had to be burned to make the lime for plastering the walls, and in time John's supporters in London sent out a bell, which was placed on a pole and used to call the people to worship each Lord's Day.

One of John's most joyful days was when on 24 October 1869, about one hundred and eighty attended worship where the Lord's Supper was dispensed to twelve islanders. Chief Namakei and his daughter Litsi were baptised when they publicly declared their love of God and saving faith in the Lord Jesus Christ.

John was overjoyed to see people who had once been murderers and cannibals sitting at the Lord's Table and taking Communion. It made all the missionaries' hard work worthwhile.

something to think about

1. John had to be sure that only true followers of Christ could become church members and sit down at the Lord's Table. What made it possible for ex-cannibals to be able to do this?

2. Both Chief Namakei's and his wife Yauwaki had poor eyesight and could not see properly until they received their spectacles (or glasses). They were both thrilled when good sight was returned to them.
    John 9 is about the healing of the blind man who received his sight when Jesus healed him. But this passage in the Bible also talks about 'spiritual blindness' - those who are 'blind' or 'cannot understand' the wonder of the Lord Jesus Christ. You may not be physically blind but you may be spiritually blind. Ask Jesus to give you 'spiritual sight'.
    Verse 25 of this passage says, 'One thing I know: that though I was blind, now I see!'

35
The Lord's Day –
and the rest of the week

The Lord's Day (or Sunday) was very busy. After a very early breakfast the ringing of the bell announced the first worship service. Nobody was ever late for the services. The bell was then rung later to announce the second service which was followed by a class for those wanting to become members of the church. John would teach those people from the catechism all that they needed to know about the Christian faith and church life. While this was going on there was a prayer meeting taking place in another building.

In the native families, at every meal the Lord was thanked for the food on the table. After lunch the bell was rung again. This told everyone that it was time for Sunday school. Here the catechism was taught to both children and adults. After lunch the missionaries, both native and European, set out to visit all the villages to preach the gospel.

By sunset everyone was back at the mission compound where drums announced the time of evening prayer. After the evening meal there would be a time of hymn and psalm singing, followed by prayer and Bible reading. At nine o'clock the villagers went home for a good night's rest, but many stayed behind to listen while John conducted family worship in English for his family.

When the classes and services were over, books were read to the children, including the native children who wanted to stay. It was a good opportunity for the family to talk to each other in English.

Sunday was a really enjoyable day, but it was also very busy. Nothing was dull or boring and John, Mary and the children spent as much time of the day together as they could.

It was not just on Sunday that life was busy; the rest of the week was as well. Very early in the morning the drums told everyone that it was time for school. School was for all ages and had to begin early to give plenty of time for work to be done in their plantations later on in the day.

People came along to read the first book printed in the Aniwan language. John and Margaret trained the people of the villages to teach others. It was only after everyone had gone home that John and the family thought about eating their breakfast.

There was a lot to be done during the rest of the day. Pages were printed on the printing-press and sick people were visited. On two days a week classes were taken by Margaret; not only for reading, writing and singing but also for sewing, where the women were taught how to make things to sell, like straw hats.

After the hard work in the plantations a swim in the sea made an enjoyable change. Next came dinner and more classes, this time for the more advanced pupils. Then while the men went fishing, the women prepared the main meal of the day which was eaten in the cool of the evening.

The day ended with the drums announcing evening prayers held under the banyan trees. It was an encouraging time for John and Margaret as they watched the Lord work in the hearts and lives of those who lived in Aniwa.

Each evening prayers were held under the banyan tree.

something to think about

1. Christians often call Sunday the 'Lord's Day'. It is God's special day of the week. What things did the people of Aniwa do on the Lord's Day to help them know more about the Lord Jesus Christ?

2. **Read Exodus 20:8.** What do you think the Bible means by 'Keeping the Sabbath Day Holy'?
   Do you ever find Sunday dull and boring? Think of some things that you could do that would help you to understand more about God and his Son.

3. Each day ended with prayers under the banyan tree. Do you end your day praying to God?

36
Changed lives

Life for the missionaries on other islands was not as secure as for John and Margaret on Aniwa. For a time after the murder of George and Ellen Gordon on the island of Erromanga there was no missionary until George's brother James went to carry on the work. He was killed when the natives blamed him for bringing diseases to the island.

A group of Erromanga Christians outside their mission station. Early in 1872 some Christian natives from Erromanga begged to be allowed to stay on Aniwa as they were afraid to return home.

On several occasions John's life was threatened, but when
he said he would leave the island, the natives took action to
end the threat.

On one occasion a man named Nourai attacked John,
hitting him again and again with the barrel of his musket until
the local women rushed in and stopped him. As the man ran
off, John told the men, who had stood by watching without
trying to intervene, 'If you do not now stop this bad conduct, I
shall leave Aniwa and go to some island where my life will be
protected.'

The next morning a party of about a hundred armed men
arrived to escort John to Nourai's village, saying, 'We will find
out why he wanted to kill you, and stop their sacred man from
pretending to cause hurricanes and diseases.'

When they arrived at the village everyone gathered round
while speeches were made on both sides. Taia, one of the men
who had accompanied John, warned the local men, 'You think
that Missi is here alone, and that you can do with him as you
please! No! We are now all Missi's men. We will fight for him
rather than see him injured. Anyone who attacks him attacks us!'

They made fun of the village sacred man, who claimed to
be able to cause hurricanes and illnesses, while suffering himself from a stiff knee. 'If he can make a hurricane, why can't he
repair the joint of his own knee?' one of them asked. 'It is surely
easier to do that than cause a hurricane!'

At that point the man's wife, who was a big, strong woman,
turned on her husband and shouted at him for bringing this
trouble on them all. Seizing a large coconut leaf, she began
hitting him on the shoulders with it, saying, 'I'll knock the Tevil
out of him! He'll not bring hurricanes again!'

Eventually John had to beg her to stop when the man promised not to cause any more trouble. Everything ended peacefully, with the villagers giving gifts of food and sugar cane to
John and his friends as a peace-offering.

On another occasion a young chief named Youwili appeared and knocked down part of the mission fence, which was the native way of declaring war. Looking at the watching natives John asked if they were going to allow one young fool to do as he pleased and stop the Lord's work on Aniwa.

Everyone gathered to decide what punishment Youwili should receive.

'Shall we kill him?' they asked.

'Certainly not,' John told them.

'What then? Shall we burn his houses and destroy his plantations? Shall we tie him up and beat him? Shall we put him in a canoe, and push it out to sea and let him drown or escape if he can?'

To all these suggestions John answered, 'No.'

As the chiefs had run out of ideas, John suggested his own:

'Make him, by himself, build a new fence; and make him promise publicly that he will stop this wicked behaviour. That will satisfy me.'

Everyone shouted out, 'It is good! It is good! Obey the word of the Missi!' So they went off to find Youwili and told him what they had decided. He was surprised to be let off so lightly and agreed.

By daybreak next morning Youwili was hard at work on the fence and by the end of the day it was repaired; in fact it was even better than before he damaged it. As he worked, some of the other natives teased him saying, 'You found it easier to cut down Missi's fence than to repair it again. You will not repeat that in a hurry!' Youwili did not answer and when the job was finished he left without saying a word.

Later Youwili became a true servant of the Lord Jesus. After attending his first communion he approached John as he had a problem: 'Missi,' he said, 'I've given up everything for Jesus, except one. I want to know if it is bad, if it will make Jesus angry; for if it does, I am willing to give it up. I want to live so as to please Jesus now. Missi, I have not yet given up my pipe and tobacco! Oh, Missi, I have used it for so long, and I do like it so well; but if you say that it makes Jesus angry with me, I will smash my pipe now and never smoke again!'

John didn't approve of smoking and always encouraged the new Christians to give it up. However, he knew that many Christians back at home in Great Britain and in Australia smoked and he did not believe it right to set a double standard.

He began by explaining his own views to Youwili: 'For my part, you know that I do not smoke; and from my point of view I would think it wrong to waste time and money and health in blowing tobacco smoke into the air.

'But,' he added, 'I must be true to you, Youwili, and admit that many of God's dear people don't agree with me. I will not therefore condemn these, our fellow-Christians, by calling smoking a sin … but I will say to you that I believe it is a foolish and wasteful habit, and that though you may serve and please Jesus with it, you might serve and please Jesus very much better without it.'

Youwili thought hard for a time and then replied, 'Missi, I give up everything else. If it won't make Jesus angry, I will keep the pipe. I have used it so long, and oh, I do like it!'

There were times when food was in short supply and everyone on the island suffered. Everyone longed for the day when a ship would arrive with supplies of food and every day a watch was kept out to sea, hoping to see the first sign of a ship arriving. When the new 'Dayspring' – a three-masted ship appeared on the horizon everyone was thrilled, especially the children who were orphans and were cared for by John and Margaret.

When the ship dropped anchor outside the coral reef, the native boats pulled alongside to bring the precious cargo to the shore. One barrel was of great interest to the children because they could tell it was full of biscuits. The asked John if they could take it to the Mission House as John had promised them biscuits when the supplies arrived.

When he returned to the mission storehouse, the children were standing around the casket. When John asked them why they had not opened the container and had their biscuit, they replied that even though they were hungry they would not eat until he had thanked God for sending them the food.

What a change God had made to the people of Aniwa.

Rolling home the barrel of biscuits

something to think about

1. Why did the children not eat the biscuits until John arrived? Do you always remember to thank God for your food?

2. Which island did the native Christians flee from because they were afraid they would be killed?

3. Youwili did not give up smoking his pipe when he became a Christian. Many people today, even children, do things that really damage their health. It may be smoking, drinking lots of alcohol or taking illegal drugs. It is very foolish and dangerous to harm our bodies in this way.
   Read 1 Corinthians 6:20. In verse **19** Paul calls our bodies 'a temple of the Holy Spirit'. Then in verse **20** he goes on to say that Christians are not their own; they have been bought with a price. Do you know who paid that price and how much it cost?

37
Passing on the baton

One of the first islanders on Aniwa to help John and Margaret was Chief Namakei. He was a great warrior, who loved war, killing and cannibalism. As the days passed he became interested in the gospel, and after the incident with the well that produced 'rain' he openly confessed his love of Missi's God and spoke of his saving faith in the Lord Jesus Christ.

That gentle old man knew that death was not far away and asked John if he could attend the next missionary conference. They were held annually and he wanted to know what was happening on the other islands. He wanted to hear the missionaries speak about their work and difficulties throughout the New Hebrides.

John knew Namakei was frail and was greatly concerned that he might not be well enough to return to Aniwa. He knew that would cause trouble on the island. However Namakei went on board the 'Dayspring' telling those who gathered to see him off: 'Be strong for Jesus and always be loyal and kind to Missi, whether I return or not.'

After a few days on Aneityum he was thrilled with what he heard and was shown great respect by everyone who met him. But after four or five days, the old chief knew he was dying and sent for John. When John arrived he said, "Missi, I will soon die! I have asked you to come and say farewell. Tell my daughter, my brother and my people to go on pleasing Jesus, and I will meet them again in the fair world.'

John told his dear Christian friend that God could still give
him the strength to get well enough to go back home to his
people but Namakei knew he was about to die. He interrupted
John in a faint whisper: 'O Missi, death is already touching me!
Help me to lie down under the shade of that banyan tree.'

The old man lay down thankfully in the cool shade of the
tree and asked John to pray with him. 'I am going!' he whis-
pered. 'O Missi, let me hear your words rising up in prayer, and
then my soul will be strong to go.'

John tried to pray, but he was so sad at the thought of losing
his dear friend – the very first of the islanders to be converted
through his work – that he could hardly get the words out.

At last Namakei took hold of John's hand, pressed it to his
heart and said, 'O my Missi, my dear Missi, I go before you, but
I will meet you again in the home of Jesus. Farewell!' With
those words on his lips Chief Namakei died peacefully. Chief
Namakei was buried in Aneityum, surrounded by all the conference delegates. John was very concerned that the natives
would blame the missionaries for his death.

As the ship drew near to Aniwa it was Namakei's daughter
who first noticed her father missing. She called out, 'Missi,
where's my father? Is Namakei dead?' John answered, 'Yes.
He died on Aneityum. He is now with Jesus in glory!'

Litsi took John aside and through her tears said, 'We knew
that he was dying but we dared not tell you. When you agreed
to let him go, he went round and said farewell to all his friends
and told them that he was going to sleep in Jesus on Aneityum,
and that at the Great Day he would rise to meet Jesus with the
glorious company of the Aneityumese Christians. He urged us
all to obey you and be true to Jesus. Truly, Missi, we will
remember my dear father's parting word and follow in his steps
and help you in the work of the Lord!'

Other chiefs took up the work of Chief Namakei and the
gospel spread throughout the island. Almost every native

attended worship each Lord's Day and confessed their faith in the Lord Jesus Christ.

Chief Naswai, another very important chief on Aniwa, was also converted and became a great warrior of the Lord Jesus. One of his greatest delights was to carry the large pulpit Bible from the mission house to the church building every Lord's Day morning.

He was also a very able preacher and made his sermons come alive by using clever illustrations drawn from his life on the island. Once, when preaching to a group from the island of Fortuna, he told them that before Christianity came to Aniwa the islanders had '...no peace and no joy in heart or house, in villages or in lands; but now they lived as brethren and have happiness in all these things.'

Naswai went on to explain that the only person who can really tell others about the Christian gospel is one who 'loves Jesus ... and walks with him and tries to please him'. Chief Naswai died in 1875 when John and Margaret were visiting Australia and New Zealand.

Chief Nerwa was the most powerful chief after Namakei and Naswai. He opposed John and the gospel, but when he was converted he became another great warrior of the Lord Jesus Christ. He took over Naswai's job of carrying the Bible to church and getting the church ready for the service.

When he knew he was dying almost every person on the island visited him. It was he who prayed with visitors and urged them to trust in the Lord.

Knowing his time was almost gone, he asked John to call the young people of the island to his bedside. He told them: 'After I am gone, let there be no bad talk, no heathen ways. Sing Jehovah's songs and pray to Jesus, and bury me as a Christian. Take good care of my Missi and help him all you can. I am dying happy and am going to be with Jesus, and it was Missi who showed me the way.'

Then he asked for a chapter of the Bible to be read and both he and John prayed. Finally, at his request, the Christians standing around his bed sang in their own language the words of the hymn, 'There is a Happy Land'.

As they did so the old man pressed John's hand and slipped peacefully away to live in the land of which they were singing.

There is a happy land,
Far, far away,
Where saints in glory stand,
Bright, bright as day.
Oh how they sweetly sing,
'Worthy is our Saviour King!'
Loud let his praises ring,
Praise, praise for aye,,,

Chief Nerwa's place as the school teacher was taken by the very girl who had been used by God to make him think seriously about God's message.

After the death of Chief Namakei, his daughter Litsi and her husband went to work on the island of Tanna, the place where John had found so much opposition when he first went to the New Hebrides. But she knew that it was Tanna where the Lord wanted her to be. It was still a place of darkness but the natives were beginning to show an interest in the gospel.

Litsi was a Chief's daughter and therefore would now be a very important person on the island of Aniwa. She missed her life on that island and wrote to John, 'My days are hard. I might be happy and independent as Queen of my own Aniwa. But the heathen here are beginning to listen. The Missi sees them coming nearer to Jesus. And oh, what a reward when we shall hear them sing and pray to our dear Saviour! The hope of that makes me strong for anything.'

For many years Litsi was part of a faithful team who worked on the island of Tanna, bringing the good news of Jesus to people who had once been such cruel warriors and cannibals.

Litsi, the daughter of Chief Namakei

A school house on Aniwa

something to think about

1. What were the last words Chief Namakei spoke. How could this old cannibal end his life with such words of trust in Jesus?

2. **Read 2 Corinthians 5:17.** Paul writes that when we become Christians 'the old has gone'. Before his conversion Paul acted in a really dreadful way towards Christians but God totally forgave him. **(Read Acts 7:54-8:3).**

3. If a relay race is run well you can hardly see the change-over of the baton. In the Bible the Christian life is often compared to a race. **Read 2 Timothy 4:7.** Paul is almost at the end of his life – he has almost finished 'running his race'. Now he is passing on the baton to Timothy. In the same way Namakei passed on the baton to his daughter Litsi. Think of some other people in the story of John Paton who 'passed on the baton'! You may want to read the next chapter before answering this question.

38
Farewell to Aniwa

John's translation and printing of many portions of the Scriptures was finished and the people had their own hymn book. The natives introduced Christian laws and punishments if they were broken. The school was functioning well and many people, especially the young, could read.

There were four children in the Paton family – Bobby, Fred, Minn and Frank. In March 1873 baby Helena (called Lena) was born but sadly died several days later. Both John and Margaret were so ill that native Christians had to dig the small grave and bury the little baby's body. It was decided that they both needed a rest and were returned to Australia. Again John was travelling about and speaking, asking for donations to assist the mission work and the provision of a new boat – the 'Paragon'.

John also made a trip to New Zealand. On board the boat were people who had been to the races in Melbourne. One of those who sat at his table, continually blasphemed the Lord's name. At last John decided to say something to protect the name of the Lord he loved: 'I am sure no man at this table wishes to wound the feelings of another or to give needless pain.'

Everyone turned and stared at him, but no one spoke as he went on: 'We are to be fellow passengers for a week or more. Now I am hurt and wounded in my heart to hear you cursing the name of my heavenly Father, and taking in vain the name of my blessed Saviour. It is God in whom we live and move; it is Jesus who died to save us, and I would rather ten times over, you would wound and abuse me, which no gentleman here would think of doing, than swear using those holy names so dear to me.' There was silence, but never again during the voyage did anyone at his table blaspheme the name of the God John served and loved.

In New Zealand Sunday school children were again encouraged to buy 'shares' in the new ship 'Dayspring II'. Money was also raised for mission work in the New Hebrides. Soon it was time for John and Margaret to return to Aniwa and take up where they had left off.

John and Margaret had worked on Aniwa for fifteen years; from 1866 to 1881. It was in August 1881 that the time came for them to permanently leave the island and become roving ambassadors for the mission.

Many tears flowed as farewells were said, but soon John and Margaret were sailing to Australia, leaving behind the graves containing two little bodies of their children – baby Lena and little Walter who had died at the age of two. The natives were sad to see them go, and Hutshi, one of the native girls said, 'You yourselves may go away, Missi, and leave us; but you can't rob us of the little ones in the graves. These two are ours; they belong to the people of Aniwa; and they will rise with the Aniwans in the great Resurrection day, and they will go with us to meet with Jesus in his glory!'

In 1884 John travelled to Great Britain, again to encourage support for the work, including a new ship to replace the 'Dayspring II'. He used his old home as a base and travelled widely throughout the nation. He so greatly missed the people of Aniwa, who were constantly on his mind that once in public prayer he commenced praying in English, but suddenly stopped and began again in the native language.

While in England he was invited to the home of the great Baptist preacher, Charles Spurgeon, who introduced him to the guests as 'John Paton – the King of the Cannibals!'

John travelled far and wide throughout the world speaking out against slavery, the sale of guns and alcohol to the native people, and creating a great interest and sympathy for mission work.

One story he loved to tell was of the night, in his early days on the island of Tanna, when the mission house was surrounded by a crowd of hostile islanders who had come to kill John and his companions. The missionaries spent time in prayer to God and in the morning they found that all the natives had gone.

Some years later John was talking to the leader of the men who had been outside the mission compound that night and asked why they had not attacked and killed everyone. The chief replied with another question: 'Who were all those men with you that night?' John was puzzled. As far as he knew there was no one outside the house that night, apart from the men who had come to attack. What exactly had happened that night would always remain a mystery, but John believed that God must have sent his angels to protect him and the other mission-aries who were praying in that little house.

John continued with the translation of the Scriptures for the people of Aniwa, and made several visits to the island. How-ever, he and Margaret settled down in Melbourne, Australia. Margaret died in 1905 and John passed away to be with the Lord on 28 January 1907, aged eighty three years.

John and Margaret were thrilled to know that two of their children had returned to the New Hebrides to carry on mission work amongst the natives – Frederick on the island of Malekula and Frank and his wife on an island which always had a very special place in John's affections – Tanna, where he himself had begun his work so many years before, and where Mary, his first wife and little Peter were buried.

Looking back over his life he wrote: 'Oh that I had my life to begin again! I would consecrate it anew to Jesus in seeking the conversion of the remaining cannibals in the New Hebrides. But since that cannot be, may he help me every moment to carry on that beloved work.'

He went on to say that the Lord had his own people, chosen and loved from eternity among these primitive and cruel tribes-men and women, and he looked forward to seeing thousands of them joining in the worship and glory of heaven.

He also praised the Lord for leading and guiding him through-out his life. He considered it to have been a wonderful privilege to have been used by God to bring the gospel to these islanders.

His closing words expressed the hope that the story of his life would be used to stir up a greater interest in the work of missions among God's people, and perhaps even to lead some of his readers to give their own lives to missionary work: 'And should the story of my poor and broken life lead anyone to give himself to mission work at home or abroad that he may win souls for Jesus, or should it even deepen the missionary spirit in those who already know and serve the Redeemer of us

all – for this also, and for all through which he has led me by his loving and gracious guidance, I shall, unto the endless ages of eternity, bless and adore my beloved Master and Saviour and Lord, to whom be glory for ever and ever.'

John G. Paton in 1894,
at the age of seventy